Muhammad Wolfgang G. A. Schmidt

Prepare Yourself for the Chinese Language Proficiency Exam (HSK)

Elementary Chinese Language Difficulty Levels

Volume I: HSK Levels 1 and 2

disserta
Verlag

Schmidt, Muhammad Wolfgang G. A.: Prepare Yourself for the Chinese Language Proficiency Exam (HSK). Elementary Chinese Language Difficulty Levels. Volume I: HSK Levels 1 and 2, Hamburg, disserta Verlag, 2019

Buch-ISBN: 978-3-95935-503-2
PDF-eBook-ISBN: 978-3-95935-504-9
Druck/Herstellung: disserta Verlag, Hamburg, 2019

Bibliografische Information der Deutschen Nationalbibliothek:
Die Deutsche Nationalbibliothek verzeichnet diese Publikation in der Deutschen Nationalbibliografie; detaillierte bibliografische Daten sind im Internet über http://dnb.d-nb.de abrufbar.

Das Werk einschließlich aller seiner Teile ist urheberrechtlich geschützt. Jede Verwertung außerhalb der Grenzen des Urheberrechtsgesetzes ist ohne Zustimmung des Verlages unzulässig und strafbar. Dies gilt insbesondere für Vervielfältigungen, Übersetzungen, Mikroverfilmungen und die Einspeicherung und Bearbeitung in elektronischen Systemen.

Die Wiedergabe von Gebrauchsnamen, Handelsnamen, Warenbezeichnungen usw. in diesem Werk berechtigt auch ohne besondere Kennzeichnung nicht zu der Annahme, dass solche Namen im Sinne der Warenzeichen- und Markenschutz-Gesetzgebung als frei zu betrachten wären und daher von jedermann benutzt werden dürften.

Die Informationen in diesem Werk wurden mit Sorgfalt erarbeitet. Dennoch können Fehler nicht vollständig ausgeschlossen werden und die Bedey Media GmbH, die Autoren oder Übersetzer übernehmen keine juristische Verantwortung oder irgendeine Haftung für evtl. verbliebene fehlerhafte Angaben und deren Folgen.

Alle Rechte vorbehalten

© disserta Verlag, Imprint der Bedey Media GmbH
Hermannstal 119k, 22119 Hamburg
http://www.disserta-verlag.de, Hamburg 2019
Printed in Germany

List of Contents

Introductory Notes *v*

Elementary Levels (HSK Level 1 & 2) *1 - 146*

HSK Level 1 *3 - 74*
Chinese Characters *5 - 38*
HSK Level 1 Charater List *7 - 8*
Chiese Characters with Hanyu Pinyin Transcription and
English Meaning Definitions *9 - 19*
HSK Level 1 Chinese Character Stroke Order *21 - 38*

Words To Know *39 - 54*

A - B *41*	P - Q *49*
C - D *42*	R - S *50*
E - F *44*	T *51*
G - H *45*	W - X *52*
J *46*	Y *53*
K - L *47*	Z *54*
M - N *48*	

Grammar Points *55 - 74*
HSK Level 1 *57*
Overview *58*
Words and Phrases *59*
Sentence Patterns *68*
Compements *72*
Suggested Further Reading *73*
References *74*

HSK Level 2 *75 - 145*
Chinese Characters *77 - 108*
HSK Level 2 Character List *79 - 80*
HSK Exam Level 2 Chinese Characters with Latin Hanyu Transcription and English Meaning Definitions *81 - 90*
HSK Level 2 - Chinese ´Character Stroke Order *91 - 108*

Words To Know *109 - 123*

B *111*	N - P *118*
C *112*	Q - R *119*
D *113*	S - T *120*
F - G *114*	W - X *121*
H - J *115*	Y *122*
K *116*	Z *123*
L - M *117*	

Grammar Points 125 - 145
HSK Level 2   127
Overview   128
Words and Phrases 129 - 137
Sentences 138 - 139
Complements   140 - 140
Complex Sentence Structures   141 - 142
Fixed Structures 143 - 143
Suggested Furthér Reading   144
References 145

Introductory Notes

While preparing for the Chinese Language Proficiency Exam (CLPE, [HSK, 汉语水平考试 *Hànyǔ Shuǐpíng Kǎoshì*]), administered by the Hanban in the People's Republic of China, you will face the issue of mastering the foreign languge (here: Chinese) via the four communicative language skills of speaking, writing, listening and reading comprehension. ´You won't be able to achieve any level of mastering such languge skills without a sound knowledge of its "material" like the knowlege of Chinese characters, their pronunciation, a certain amount of vocabulary acquired and following an essential set of grammatical rules. This book in your hands will cover all the necssary material that is needed as a pre-requisite for masterin the four communicative languages skills. In other words, you will find here all the essential material covering Chinese characters, vocabulary and Grammar Points enabling you to communicate effectively and efficiently by making use of the four communicative language skills up to a level that is relevant for your appropriate level of chosen from among the six difficulty levels of the CLPE (HSK).

Fig. 1 demonstrates this inter-relationship between these four communicative language skills and the basic "material" underlying them:

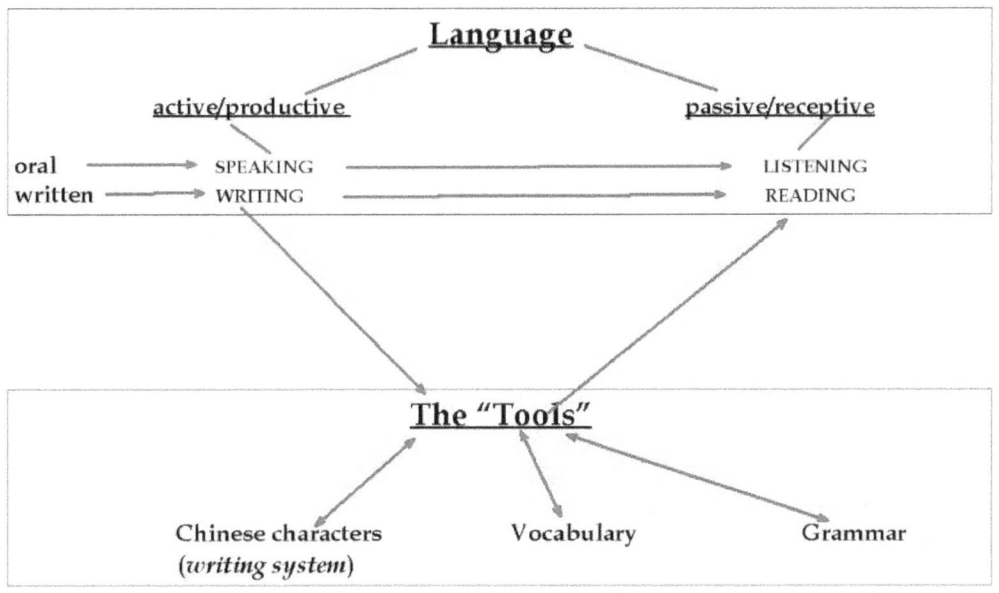

Figure 1

The system of the six difficulty levels of the CLPE (HSK) itself is organised and defined in terms of the three basic difficulty levels *Elementary*, *Intemediate* and *Advanced*. These three basic difficulty levels again are sub-divided into respective "sub-levels" like *Elementary 1* and *2*, *Intermediate 1* and *2*, and *Advanced 1* and *2*. "1" and "2" generally stand here for the sub-levels of "Lower" and "Upper" with respect to the three basic language difficulty levels *Elementary*, *Intermediate* and *Advanced*, respectively.

Hene, we have a differentiation system of *Lower* and *Upper Elementary, Intermediate* and *Advanced* language difficulty levels in foreign language learning and teaching, now also to be applied to CHINESE AS A FOREIGN LANGUAGE.

Fig. 2 indicates these languages difficuilty levels and relates them to the difficulty levels of the CLPE (HSK) and the Common European Framework of Reference for Languages (CEFR) in the following way:

Language Skill Level	*Division into Lower and Upper Level*	**HSK**	**CEFRL***
Elementary	*Lower*	HSK level 1	A1
	Upper	HSK level 2	A2
Intermediate	*Lower*	HSK level 3	B1
	Upper	HSK level 4	B2
Advanced	*Lower*	HSK level 5	C1
	Upper	HSK level 6	C2

* *Common European Framework of Reference for Languages*

Figure 2

Based on this division, we have divided and organised the material of Chinese characters, vocabulary and Grammar Points to be mstered for each of the six language difficulty levels of the CLPE into three volumes, each of them covering the language material for two language difficulty levels of the CLPE:

- Volume I covers the HSK Levels 1 and 2 and is thus called *the Elementary HSK Level*.
- Volume II covers the HSK Levels 3 and 4 and is called the *Intermediate HSK Level*.
- Volume III covers the HSK Levels 5 and 6 and is consequently called the *Advanced HSK Level*.

In each of these three volumes and for each of the two HSK language difficulty levels covered there, the followiung material is presented in depth:

- Chinese Characters
- Vocabulary
- Grammar Points

We will now deal with these three sections in more detail and explain the organisation of the material in each of them.

Chinese Characters

Generally, Chinese characters for each HSL Level are presented according to their individual number of strokes. We hope that this sorting will assist in effectively memorising them for active and passive language use in communication practice. For those HSK Level units with an inventory of over 250 Chinese unique characters set, the number of characters were sub-divided into parts such as HSK 4A, HSK 4B, HSK 4C, etc. HSK distribution of Chinese characters and their sub-divisions according to individual stroke number for each HSK difficulty level are shown in Figure 3 below.

HSK Level	Parts	Strokes	Amount of Unique Hanzi
1	-	1 - 15 strokes	178
2	-	3 - 16 Strokes	171
3	-	2 - 16 strokes	274
4	4A	1 - 8 strokes	Total: 452 4A: 177
	4B	8 - 11 strokes	4B: 180
	4C	11 - 19 strokes	4C: 95
5	5A	1 - 8 strokes	Total: 636 5A: 178
	5B	8 - 10 strokes	5B: 174
	5C	10 - 13 strokes	5C: 179
	5D	13 - 23 strokes	5D: 102
6	6A	3 - 8 strokes	Total: 924 6A: 179
	6B	8 - 9 strokes	6B: 179
	6C	9 - 11 strokes	6C: 179
	6D	11 - 13 strokes	6D: 179
	6E	13 - 22 strokes	6E: 209

Figure 3

Each section on Chinese characters covers the following:

- *Character Lists* for each HSK difficulty level. This listing will help you to see which characters are included for each respective HSK exam level, and you can test yoursel at a first glance which of them are already known to you and do not present any problems in writing and comprehension. This "pre-selection" then would enable you to concenrate on those not yet known and to pay special attention to them.

- *Chinese - English Character Glossaries* for each HSK difficulty level again follow the same principle of order arrangement acording to the individual number of strokes of these characters liste in the inventory for each HSK level. These glossaries contain information on pronunciation of characters in Hanyu Pinyin transcription followed by English Meaning definitions.

- *Stroke Order of Chinese Characters* for each HSK Level allow you to practice the writing of Chinese characters by drawig along the shaded lines with a thin pencil in the stroke order section. The lay-out of these worksheets is explained in more detail below (Figure 4).

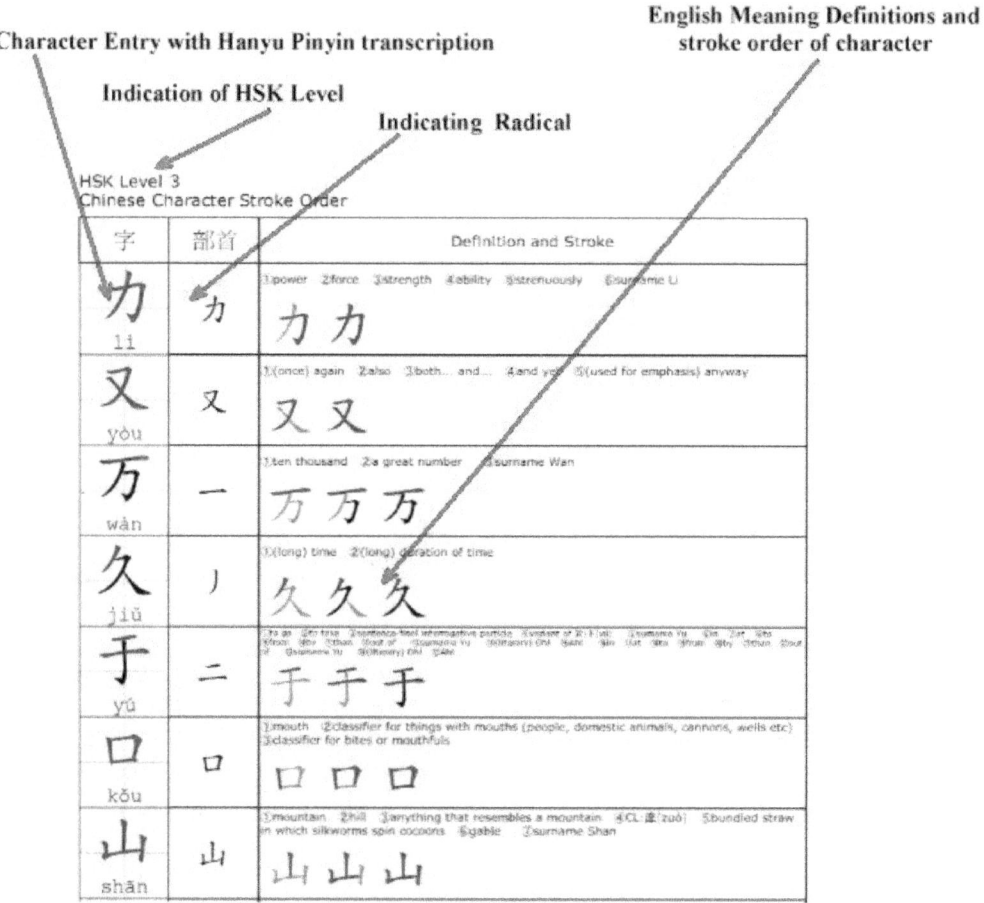

Figure 4

Note that for all those sections in the Chinese Character parts of the book, the principles arrangement of characters is the same in sequence: Sorting is acording to their individual number of strokes, with those lower in stroke number listed first and followed by those higher in number of their respective individual number of strokes. This way of sorting is also advantageous if you need to locate a certain character in any of these sections.

Vocabulary

In this part of the book, you will deal with *words* instead of *characters*. This disctinction is important in terms of Chinese grammar and Linguistic Science of Chinese. Since Chinese characters carry meaning, they easily may be confused with words from a Western point of view. In the early days of modern Chinese Linguistics, this distinction was a matter of debate among scholars and led to the conclusion that the traditional Western framework of grammar was not applicable here and that a separate graar framework was needed for the Chinese language beause of its extreme divergence in comparison to the larger family of Indo-European languages.

Word entries in this part of the book are listed alphabetically according to their transcription in Hanyu Pinyin as the following sampe extract from Volume II for HSK Level 3 indicates (Figure 5).

Words To Know

A

阿姨 āyí ◊ {colloquial} auntie (mother's sister) ◊ auntie (term of address for a woman of one's parent's generation) ◊ {Mainland usage} (in a home) nanny, nursemaid, housekeeper; (in a nursery school or kindergarten) childcare worker
阿 ā ◊ {regional} dear...(name prefix, used to form terms of endearment; prefix before a kinship term) ◊ Afghanistan (short form for Āfūhàn 阿富汗) ◊ A (surname)
矮 ǎi ◊ short (in stature), low (in height) ◊ inferior to
爱好 àihào ◊ hobby, an activity one likes ◊ like, love, be fond of, be keen on
安静 ānjìng ◊ quiet, calm, noiseless ◊ peaceful

B

把 bǎ ◊ {grammar} take... (and do sth with it) (auxiliary verb used to introduce the direct object of a sentence in front of the main verb) ◊ hold, grasp, grip ◊ hold (a baby out to relieve itself) ◊ grab, control, monopolize ◊ {sports, colloquial} guard, watch (like a goal) ◊ {colloquial} be close to ◊ hold sth together ◊ {regional} give, offer ◊ handlebar (like of a bicycle) ◊ bunch, bundle, handful ◊ {measure word} (used for tools and other things with a handle, like key, scissors, umbrella, sword, etc., or for things that can be grasped [chair], or for certain abstract things [years, strength, effort], a movement of the hands [like a push, a helping hand]) ◊ "approximately" (when following numerals/measure words, like bǎi bǎ nián 百把年 "approx. 100 years") ◊ refers to sworn brotherhood (as in bàibǎzi 拜把子 "become sworn brothers")
班 bān ◊ (of school) class, grade ◊ (of airline) flight ◊ shift, duty, work

Figure 5

The arrangement of data in this part of the book is largely self-explanatory and does not require any further comments.

Grammar Points

Again, the arrangement of the material in this last part of the book is largely self-explanatory and does not require any further comment. The *Overview* in this part of the book lists all the important grammar points required for each HSK exam level (Figure 6 below; sample extract below is taken from the HSK 6 Grammar Point part in Volume III).

Overview

Words and Phrases
1. **Nouns:** 以来

2. **Verbs**
2.1 多亏
2.2 靠

3. **Adjectives** : 难免

4. **Adverbs**
4.1 便
4.2 根本
4.3 果然
4.4 忽然
4.5 简直
4.6 连忙
4.7 难怪
4.8 始终
4.9 勿

5. **Prepositions**
5.1 朝
5.2 趁
5.3 于
5.4 至于

6. **Conjunctions:** 以及

7. **Particles**

7.1 似的
7.2 所

Sentences
8. **Special Sentence Patterns**
8.1 Pivotal Sentences
8.1.1 令
8.1.2 派
8.2 Sentences of Comparison: A不如B (这么/那么) + Adjective

Complex Sentences
9. **Complex Sentences**
9.1   不但不/不但没有。。。, 反而。。。
9.2 Other Complex Structures I
9.2.1 宁可。。。, 也不/也要。。。
9.2.2 与其。。。, 不如。。。
9.3. Other Complex Structures II
9.3.1 假如。。。, 就。。。
9.3.2 万。。。, (就)。。。
9.3.3 (幸亏)。。。, 不然。。。
9.4 除非。。。, 不然。。。
9.5 哪怕。。。, 也/还。。。

Fixed Structures
10. **Fixed Structures:** 为。。。所

Suggested Further Reading

Figure 6

汉语水平考试

Elementary 1 and 2

HSK Levels 1 and 2

汉语水平考试

HSK Level 1

汉语水平考试

汉字

Chinese Characters

HSK Level 1 Character List

和国姐学店明朋服杯果爸狗现的苹视话雨亮前哪客很怎星昨是点看茶觉语说钟院面

多她好妈字岁师年有机欢米老衣西那住作你冷医听坐块我时来没系识这里饭些京呢

日月气水火见认车东他们写出北去叫四对打本汉生电买会先关兴再吃同名后吗回在

一七九了二人儿八几十三上下个么习大女子小工飞不中书五什今六分午友天太少开

睡零漂影

猫菜馆喂喜喝期椅谢想

脑请读谁起都钱高做商

候家校样桌热爱租站能

HSK Level 1
Chinese Character List with Latin Hanyu Pinyin and English Meaning Definitions

一 yī ◊ one, 1 ◊ alone ◊ whole ◊ once... ◊ Yi (surname)

七 qī ◊ seven, 7 ◊ {Buddhism} sacrifices held every seven days after death until the forty-ninth day ◊ rhyming prose ◊ Qi (surname)

九 jiǔ ◊ nine, 9 ◊ {Chinese calendar} any of the nine-day periods starting the day after the winter solstice ◊ many, numerous

了 le ◊ already (aspect particle indicating change) ◊ (aspect particle for new situation; verb suffix indicating an action has happened or is about to happen)

二 èr ◊ two, 2; second; double; dual; binary ◊ second in charge/command, etc., sub-, vice- ◊ {colloquial} slow-witted, flaky ◊ comparable peer, equal ◊ different ◊ doubt, hesitate ◊ change

人 rén ◊ person(s), human being(s), people, man ◊ somebody else, the others ◊ Ren (surname)

儿 ér ◊ child, baby, son (written as "r" when used as a suffix, indicates smallness [e.g., màor 帽兒/帽儿 "hat"]; after a verb/adjective turns it into a noun [e.g., chīr 吃兒/吃儿 "eatables, food"]; added to a concrete noun turns it into an abstract noun [e.g., ménr 門兒/门儿 "work"]; added to a noun to change its original meaning [e.g., báimiànr 白麵兒/白面儿 means "heroin", while báimiàn 白麵/白面 means "white flour"]; used as suffix to certain verbs [e.g., wánr 玩兒/玩儿 "play"])

八 bā ◊ eight, 8 (note on pronunciation: when followed by a word in the fourth tone, the reading of bā 八 changes to bá [second tone])

几 jǐ ◊ How many? ◊ a few, several, some

十 shí ◊ ten, tenth ◊ complete ◊ perfect

三 sān ◊ three, 3 ◊ several, numerous, many (the character 叁 is also used in Simplified character mode, to avoid forgery)

上 shàng ◊ on, on top of... ◊ last, the previous (like shàng [gè] xīngqīwǔ 上[個]星期五 "last Friday") ◊ first (in a series) ◊ go up, go up to ◊ mount, board (a vehicle) ◊ go to, leave for ◊ submit, send ◊ bolt, lock (a door, etc.) ◊ (used after a verb as a resultative ending to indicate the amount or extent reached)

下 xià ◊ under, below, underneath ◊ the later, latter, last in a series ◊ the last part (of a work) ◊ next ◊ down, downward ◊ descend, go down ◊ (of rain, snow, etc.) fall ◊ send down (like documents); issue, deliver (like an order, an ultimatum, etc.) ◊ leave/exit (from) ◊ put in ◊ play (board games) ◊ take away, dismantle ◊ (of animals) give birth to, lay (eggs) ◊ defeat, capture ◊ yield, give up, give in ◊ get off/finish (one's shift) ◊ {measure word} (used for the number of occurrences) ◊ {measure word}... glassful(s) of... (used for fillings of containers like glasses, bowls, etc.)

个 gè ◊ {measure word} (usually pronounced in the qīngshēng 輕聲/轻声 "light tone") (used before a noun not having a dedicated measure word of its own, e.g., sān gè xīngqī 三個星期/三个星期 "three weeks", liǎng gè wèntí 兩個問題/两个问题 "two questions/problems") ◊ (contraction of yī gè 一個/一个, used between a verb and its object) a... ◊ (pronounced with full fourth tone) individual

么 me ◊ (a suffix, as in shénme 甚麼/什么 "what?")

习 xí ◊ practice, exercise ◊ be used to, be familiar with ◊ practice, custom, habit ◊ hover, circle (in flight)

◇ Xi (surname)

大 dà ◇ big, large, great ◇ greatly, to a large extent, in a major way ◇ major, important, main ◇ general strong, heavy ◇ loud, high (like volume of sound, or sb's voice) ◇ (of persons) old (i.e. of a certain age) ◇ the oldest (among two or more) ◇ adult, elder ◇ (as emphatic prefix) even on...(followed by a time expression, as in dà Xīngqīrì 大星期日 "even on Sundays") ◇ (as honorific prefix) your... ◇ (used for transcription of the syllable -da- in foreign names) ◇ Da (surname)

女 nǚ ◇ woman, female ◇ girl, daughter ◇ {Chinese astronomy} Nü (Nǚ Xiù 女宿 "Nü constellation", one of the Èrshíbā Xiù 二十八宿 "28 Lunar Mansions of the Chinese zodiac")

子 zǐ ◇ son, child ◇ person ◇ (of melons, etc.) seed ◇ (of fowl, fish) egg, roe ◇ sth small and hard (pebble, bead, etc.) ◇ sub(ordinate) ◇ (in Chinese chess) a chess piece ◇ {history} viscount (the fourth of the five ranks of nobility) ◇ {respectful address} master, sir; Master... (suffix added to the names of ancient philosophers, such as Kǒngzǐ 孔子 "Confucius", Mèngzǐ 孟子 "Mencius") ◇ zi (first of the twelve Dìzhī 地支 "Earthly Branches") ◇ zi (11:00 p.m. to 1:00 a.m.; one of the twelve two-hour periods in a day) ◇ Zi (surname)

小 xiǎo ◇ small, little ◇ my dear...(when used as [endearment] prefix, it can partially or totally lose its original meaning of "small")

工 gōng ◇ work, labour; worker, labourer ◇ (construction/engineering) project ◇ industry ◇ (short for gōngchéngshī 工程師/工程师) engineer ◇ man-day ◇ craftsmanship, workmanship, skill ◇ be expert at, be good at, be versed in, be skilled in (like the arts) ◇ excellent, exquisite ◇ {Chinese music} "gōng" (3rd note in the traditional Chinese musical scale gōngchěpǔ 工尺譜/工尺谱); musician

飞 fēi ◇ (of birds, airplanes, etc.) fly ◇ hover, soar or flutter in the air swiftly, quickly, rapidly ◇ volatilize, be vapourized ◇ (of disaster, misfortune, examination) unexpected, sudden, random; (of slander) baseless, unfounded ◇ {colloquial} throw (sth) at (sb) ◇ {regional} (of a bicycle) free-wheel

不 bù ◇ not ◇ no

中 zhōng ◇ centre, middle ◇ in, in the middle of, amid, among ◇ medium, intermediate ◇ midsize ◇ intermediary ◇ fit for, suitable for, good for ◇ [ZH-] Chinese, Sino- ◇ the second (in a series of three) ◇ {colloquial} all right, okay ◇ in the process of, in the course of ◇ Zhong (surname)

书 shū ◇ book ◇ letter, document ◇ calligraphy style, script ◇ write ◇ {literature} the Book of Documents (short for Shàngshū 尚書/尚书, or Shūjīng 書經/书经)

五 wǔ ◇ five, 5 ◇ Wu (surname)

什 shén ◇ various, miscellaneous ◇ a group of ten (soldiers, etc.); ten

今 jīn ◇ today ◇ this (year, day, etc.) ◇ present-day, modern, contemporary ◇ now, at the present

六 liù ◇ six ◇ {music} Liu (a note on the Chinese musical scale gōngchěpǔ 工尺譜/工尺谱) ◇ Liu (surname)

分 fēn ◇ separate, divide, split, part ◇ distribute, assign, allot ◇ distinguish, differentiate, tell (the difference), make a distinction ◇ (of an organization, company, etc.) branch ◇ fraction; one-tenth of the whole, ten percent ◇ (as a unit of length) approx. 1/3 cm ◇ (as a unit of area) approx. 67 square metres ◇ (as a unit of weight) approx. 1/2 gram ◇ (as a unit of Chinese currency) 1/100 of a Yuan ◇ (as a unit of time or degree) a minute ◇ (as interest rate) percent ◇ (in a marking system) a mark/point ◇ {measure word}... part(s) of...,... tenth(s) of... (used for parts or tenths of the whole, and for abstract items like vigour, toil, hope, etc.)

午 wǔ ◇ noon ◇ wu (seventh of the twelve dìzhī 地支 "Earthly Branches") ◇ wu (11:00 a.m. to 1:00 p.m., one of the twelve two-hour periods of time) ◊ Wu (surname)

友 yǒu ◊ friend, ally; friendly; befriend ◊ fraternal affection

天 tiān ◊ day ◊ sky ◊ weather ◊ the heavens ◊ Tian (surname)

太 tài ◊ too, excessively ◊ so, extremely (used in an exclamatory clause) ◊ greatest, highest ◊ Tai (surname)

少 shǎo ◊ few, little, less, scant, not enough ◊ seldom ◊ missing, lacking ◊ owe (money, etc.) ◊ a (little) while, a minute

开 kāi ◊ open, open up, reclaim ◊ turn on (a light, the TV, a switch, etc.), be on ◊ operate, run (a machine, etc.) ◊ boil (water), boiled (water) ◊ lift (a restriction, ban, etc.) ◊ (of troops) move (in...) ◊ start, begin, set up (like a restaurant, shop, etc.) ◊ hold (a meeting, party, etc.) ◊ write, make out (like a prescription, receipt) ◊ pay (wages, a salary, etc.) ◊ (of a waterway) thaw, become navigable ◊ {regional} kick out, sack, fire ◊ (as a verb suffix)... far and wide; start (doing sth) ◊ rough percentage, approximate proportion ◊ {printing} folio (unit of paper size) ◊ Kai (surname)

日 rì ◊ sun ◊ day, daytime ◊ daily, on a daily basis, every day ◊ the days, time ◊ (short for Rìběn 日本) Japan; Japanese

月 yuè ◊ month ◊ moon ◊ Yue (surname)

气 qì ◊ gas, air ◊ power ◊ vigour, spirit ◊ weather, climate ◊ thin clouds ◊ make angry ◊ get angry ◊ fate, destiny ◊ {Chinese philosophy} formative or creative spirit ◊ {Chinese med} qi, vital energy; functions (of internal organs); symptom (of a disease); nutrition

水 shuǐ ◊ water ◊ (preceded by a name) ... River ◊ rivers, lakes, seas; a flood ◊ liquid ◊ additional income; extra cost ◊ (of clothing, etc.) times being washed ◊ Shui (surname)

火 huǒ ◊ fire ◊ firearms, ammunition ◊ {Chinese med} internal heat ◊ (of colour) red as fire, flaming red ◊ urgent, pressing ◊ anger, fury, rage, temper ◊ {colloquial} (of business, a sales item, etc.) brisk, flourishing, thriving, popular, "hot", all the rage (as in shēngyì hěn huǒ 生意很火 "business is booming", or mài de tǐng huǒ 賣得挺火/卖得挺火 "[some product] is selling like hotcakes") ◊ Huo (surname)

见 jiàn ◊ see, perceive ◊ be exposed to, come in contact with, meet with, call on ◊ show evidence of, appear/seem to be ◊ view, opinion, understanding ◊ {written} (as a particle, when preceding a verb indicates the passive voice, or the request towards sb to do sth for the writer)

认 rèn ◊ recognize, know, distinguish ◊ admit, acknowledge ◊ adopt ◊ enter into/establish a relationship

车 chē ◊ vehicle, car ◊ implement or machine containing rotating elements (like a spinning wheel, water wheel, windmill) ◊ machine, turn on a lathe ◊ draw/lift water with a water wheel ◊ {dialect} carry (away) in a vehicle ◊ {dialect} sew sth on a sewing machine ◊ turn (one's body) ◊ Che (surname)

东 dōng ◊ east ◊ owner, master ◊ host ◊ Dong (surname)

他 tā ◊ he, she, it ◊ him, his (personal pronoun, prior to the May Fourth Movement [1919] used for all genders; now generally only used in reference to males, in cases when no gender differentiation is necessary, or when the gender is unknown; this is also the standard usage in Taiwan) ◊ other, another (as in tārì 他日 "on another day")

们 men ◊ (suffix added to pronouns or personal nouns to indicate the plural, e.g., wǒmen 我們/我们 "we"; rénmen 人們/人们 "people"; used for humans only)

写 xiě ◊ write, compose ◊ draw, paint, sketch ◊ portray, depict

出 chū ◊ go out, exit, come out, come from ◊ give out, issue, offer ◊ occur, happen, arise, emerge, show, ap-

pear ◊ produce, turn out, yield ◊ publish ◊ vent (like one's anger) ◊ expend, pay (out), spend ◊ {measure word} (used for theatrical or acrobatic performances, plays, readings, etc.) ◊ {regional} (suffix indicating direction of movement) ◊ (as verb ending) out
北 běi ◊ north ◊ go north ◊ toward the north, northward ◊ be defeated
去 qù ◊ go (to), go away, leave, depart ◊ get rid of, remove ◊ (verb suffix indicating movement to a place)
叫 jiào ◊ shout, yell, cry ◊ call out to, greet, address ◊ hire (like a taxi), order (a meal, dish, etc.), get ◊ name, call, designate, summon; be called/named ◊ ask, order, make (sb do sth), order, ask ◊ allow, permit, let ◊ by (particle used to indicate the passive voice) ◊ {regional} male (animal or fowl)
四 sì ◊ four, 4 ◊ Si (surname)
对 duì ◊ toward, to, facing, regarding ◊ be directed at, confront, treat, cope with ◊ opposite ◊ couple, pair (usually a man and a woman) ◊ {measure word}... pair(s) of... (used for things that come in pairs, like shoes, or for abstract dualities, as in yī duì máodùn 一對矛盾/一对矛盾 "a contradiction") ◊ agree, fit ◊ compare, identify, check ◊ set, adjust, synchronize (like clocks) ◊ pair up, fit together, coordinate ◊ correct, right ◊ adulterate, mix with, add, dilute (like wine with water) ◊ split in half (like profit) ◊ {literature, poetry} couplet
打 dǎ ◊ strike, hit, beat ◊ break, smash, wreck ◊ batter, attack, fight ◊ come into contact with, deal with (as in dǎ jiāodao 打交道 "have dealings with") ◊ build, construct ◊ forge (like a knife) ◊ pack (like luggage) ◊ apply (like paint) ◊ make (like a phone call) ◊ remove (as in the medical term dǎchóng 打蟲/打虫 "deworm") ◊ knit, weave ◊ take/board (a train, plane) ◊ take/get/hire (a taxi) ◊ ladle, fetch (like porridge, water) ◊ hunt/catch (as in dǎyú 打魚/打鱼 "catch fish") ◊ shoot (with a fire-arm) ◊ collect, gather (like firewood) ◊ draft (a document, estimate, etc.) ◊ do (like odd jobs) ◊ label as, charge with ◊ fight (a war, battle) ◊ play (a game, sport) ◊ buy ◊ be about, concern ◊ {colloquial} (used like cóng 從/从) from; (used like cóng 從/从... qǐ 起) beginning at...
本 běn ◊ book ◊ {measure word}... volume(s) of...(used for books, scripts, reels of film, etc.) ◊ root, stem (of a plant) ◊ origin, basis, foundation ◊ {finance} capital, principal ◊ original ◊ one's own, native, home ◊ present, current, this ◊ originally ◊ edition ◊ script (of a play) ◊ memorial to the Emperor
汉 Hàn ◊ China, Chinese ◊ Han nationality (majority ethnic group in China) ◊ man ◊ Han (a dynasty, 206 BCE-220 CE)
生 shēng ◊ give birth to ◊ live ◊ life ◊ unripe ◊ raw ◊ bear, deliver ◊ generate ◊ be born ◊ (of plants, roots, etc.) grow, emerge ◊ unripe ◊ raw, undercooked ◊ not cooked ◊ unprocessed, unrefined ◊ unfamiliar, unacquainted ◊ student (bound form, as in nǚshēng 女生 "female student", zhèngshìshēng 正式生 "regular student") ◊ suffix for various kinds or groups of people (like yīshēng 醫生/医生 "medical doctor") ◊ Sheng (surname)
电 diàn ◊ electricity, (electric) power ◊ lightning ◊ receive an electric shock ◊ {IT} telegram, cable ◊ send a telegram/cable
买 mǎi ◊ buy, purchase
会 huì ◊ meeting ◊ meet with ◊ can, could ◊ understand, know (like a language) ◊ be able to ◊ will, be likely to, be possible, possibly ◊ moment, short while ◊ Hui (surname)
先 xiān ◊ first, early, earlier, in advance ◊ for the time being ◊ deceased, late ◊ ancestors, forefathers, previous generations ◊ Xian (surname)
关 guān ◊ close, shut (a door, window, etc.) ◊ turn/switch off (the lights, the TV, etc.) ◊ shut in, lock up, confine (a bird in a cage, a person in

jail, etc.) ◊ close down (a store, business, etc.) ◊ guard/defense post, mountain pass (or other place of strategic importance); the area outside the city gate ◊ bolt, bar (of a door or gate) ◊ customs house, checkpoint, barrier, juncture ◊ key, crucial ◊ {figurative} crucial point ◊ involve, concern, implicate ◊ {history} pay (wages) ◊ Guan (surname)

兴 xīng ◊ thriving, prosperous, flourishing ◊ thrive, prosper, flourish ◊ become popular/fashionable ◊ start, begin, found ◊ mobilize, call into action ◊ {literature} stand up, get up, rise ◊ {regional} allow, permit, let (mostly used with the negative) ◊ {regional} perhaps, maybe, probably ◊ Xing (surname)

再 zài ◊ again, once more ◊ further, more ◊ time and again, repeatedly ◊ no matter how... (followed by an adjective or verb, usually with dōu 都 or yě 也 in the following clause)

吃 chī ◊ eat, take/have a meal, dine ◊ live on, live off, scrounge off ◊ soak up, absorb, take in ◊ wipe out, annihilate, eat up ◊ understand, grasp ◊ suffer, incur, endure, bear, withstand ◊ consume, exhaust (like one's energy) ◊ {grammar} by (particle indicating the passive voice)

同 tóng ◊ with, together (with) ◊ identical, the same ◊ be the same as ◊ similar, alike ◊ Tong (surname)

名 míng ◊ (personal) name ◊ fame, reputation ◊ famous, well-known ◊ {measure word} (used for persons of a certain category, profession, etc.)

后 hòu ◊ after, behind ◊ back, rear ◊ afterwards, later ◊ last, in the back, at the end ◊ offspring, progeny ◊ {Chinese chess} at the rear (the piece at the rear, relative to the player) ◊ Hou (surname)

吗 ma ◊ "Is it...?" (sentence-final question particle)

回 huí ◊ return, go or come back ◊ wind around, circle/turn around, look back ◊ answer, reply ◊ report (to a higher authority) ◊ go contrary to, cancel, dismiss, decline (an invitation, offer, etc.) ◊ {measure word}... times (for the number of occurrences, times, occasions, etc.); {measure word} (used for chapters, sections, sessions [of books, etc.], matters, occasions) ◊ the Hui (Muslim) nationality ◊ Hui (surname)

在 zài ◊ in, on, at ◊ exist, be present, be alive ◊ be in a certain category or class (as in zài suǒ bùmiǎn 在所不免 "is [one of those things that is] unavoidable") ◊ Zai (surname)

多 duō ◊ many, much; more, further; in excess, extra, exceeding (the intended/normal/original number or amount) ◊ a lot, ample ◊ (following a numeral) more than..., over (the number/amount stated) ◊ far more, much more ◊ mostly, for the most part ◊ (in questions asking about number, size, etc.) how (much, big, etc.)? ◊ (in exclamations) how...! ◊ Duo (surname)

她 tā ◊ she (third person singular, feminine) ◊ her ◊ {formal} she (as a reference to one's country, party, flag, etc.)

好 hǎo ◊ good, nice, fine ◊ good to (eat, etc.) ◊ be well, in good health ◊ (before a verb) easy to... ◊ (as a verb complement, indicates finishing or finishing satisfactorily) be done...ing, finish...ing ◊ in order to, so that, for the purpose of ◊ {regional} may, can, should, ought to ◊ (emphasizes the meaning of adjectives) very, quite, pretty much... ◊ (used before adjectives to inquire about quantity or degree) how...(long, far, etc.)?

妈 mā ◊ mother, mom

字 zì ◊ {linguistics} Chinese character, word, letter ◊ "style name" (name taken by a man upon reaching manhood, at around 20 years of age)

岁 suì ◊ year ◊ years (old), years of age ◊ the year's harvest

师 shī ◊ teacher, master ◊ example, model ◊ model (oneself after), imitate ◊ professional, skilled or specialized worker (like doctor, engineer) ◊ {military} division ◊ troops ◊ mul-

titude of people ◊ (various official titles) ◊ {divination} Shi (one of the sixty-four hexagrams in the Yìjīng 易經/易经 "Book of Changes") ◊ Shi (surname)
年 nián ◊ year ◊ yearly, annual ◊ age ◊ period of life (like childhood, middle age) ◊ age, period (of history) ◊ harvest ◊ New Year, lunisolar New Year season ◊ (of special items) for the (lunisolar) New Year (like cakes, painting) ◊ (of friendship, etc.) between those who passed the Imperial examinations in the same year ◊ Nian (surname)
有 yǒu ◊ there is (are, were, etc.); be there, exist ◊ have, own, possess ◊ You (surname)
机 jī ◊ a machine, engine ◊ an aircraft, plane ◊ an opportunity, chance, occasion ◊ {chem, food} organic ◊ important business/affairs (like affairs of state) ◊ an intention, idea ◊ smart, clever
欢 huān ◊ happy, joyous, merry ◊ sweetheart, lover; (term of affection used by females when speaking of their lover) ◊ {dialect} lively, vigorously, in full swing, with a vengeance, with great drive ◊ Huan (surname)
米 mǐ ◊ (hulled) rice ◊ {unit of measure} metre ◊ Mi (surname)
老 lǎo ◊ old, aged ◊ senior person, elderly person ◊ experienced, veteran, seasoned ◊ of long standing, old ◊ old-fashioned, outdated, obsolete ◊ former, original, same ◊ always, constantly, frequently ◊ overgrown, tough, stringy (like of vegetables that were too mature when picked; in contrast to nèn 嫩 "tender") ◊ tough, leathery, overstewed, overcooked (like of overcooked meat, well-cooked eggs, etc.) ◊ {chem} deteriorate, age, change in quality ◊ always, constantly ◊ (prefix to names to indicate affection, respect or familiarity) ◊ the venerable... (title used following a surname to indicate respect for an elderly person of superior achievements) ◊ long, for a long time ◊ very, extremely, awfully, terribly ◊ {regional} (followed by certain colours) dark... ◊ (euphemism, always followed by le 了) die ◊ Laozi (short for Lǎozǐ 老子, the Taoist philosopher) ◊ Lao (surname)
衣 yī ◊ clothes, clothing ◊ outer coating, covering ◊ feathers ◊ peel, skin, shell (of fruit) ◊ {med} placenta, afterbirth ◊ Yi (surname)
西 xī ◊ west; western, occidental; the West, the Occident ◊ {phonetic} (Xī) (short for Xībānyá 西班牙) Spain; Spanish ◊ Xi (surname)
那 nà ◊ that (one) ◊ then, in that case
住 zhù ◊ live, dwell, reside ◊ residential ◊ lodge, stay at (as in an inn) ◊ stop, halt, cease ◊ {grammar} verb complement indicating that the action of the verb has been securely obtained, completed, etc. ◊ verb complement used after "de 得" (be able to...) and after "bu 不" (not be able to...)
作 zuò ◊ do, make, work ◊ rise, grow ◊ be, become, serve as, act as ◊ engage (in an activity) ◊ compose, write; the writings, works ◊ feign, pretend ◊ consider to be, regard as ◊ feel
你 nǐ ◊ you (second person, singular) ◊ one, anyone, a person
冷 lěng ◊ cold ◊ icy, cold, frosty ◊ Leng (surname)
医 yī ◊ doctor, physician ◊ medicine, medical science ◊ treat, cure, heal
听 tīng ◊ hear, listen ◊ obey, heed, comply with, take sb's advice/suggestion ◊ administer (affairs of state, justice), manage ◊ allow, permit (formerly pronounced "tìng") ◊ sb's ears/informer ◊ {measure word, phonetic}... tin(s) of...,... can(s) of... (from the English "tin"; used for items in tin containers or cans, like biscuits, cigarettes, beer, etc.)
坐 zuò ◊ sit ◊ travel by, go by (car, airplane, etc.) ◊ (of a building, etc.) be situated/located ◊ sink, subside ◊ put a pot, kettle, pan, etc. on a fire/stove ◊ because, for the reason that... ◊ {archaic} be punished ◊ bear fruit ◊ become ill ◊ spontaneously,

naturally

块 kuài ◊ piece, lump ◊ {measure word}... piece(s)/lump(s) of... (used for money, things that come in a piece, and various thin and flat objects) ◊ "Yuan", "Dollar", etc. (unit of Chinese currency) ◊ {colloquial, business/administrative jargon} area, matter, aspect (e.g., wǎngshàng xiāoshòu zhè yī kuài 網上銷售這一塊/网上销售这一块, "the area of online sales")

我 wǒ ◊ I, me; my ◊ {written} we; our ◊ {written} our country (usu. referring to China); our country's self ◊ Wo (surname)

时 shí ◊ time ◊ when, at (a certain time) ◊ o'clock (written form) ◊ current, present ◊ at that time ◊ occasionally, now and then; at times, sometimes (in the pattern 時...時...) ◊ Shi (surname)

来 lái ◊ come, come hither ◊ arrive (of seasons, etc.) ◊ arise, crop up (of problems, etc.) ◊ cause to come, let come, I'll have... (used in ordering in a restaurant) ◊ cause to arrive or take place ◊ for the past (amount of time) ◊ in order to (take some action) ◊ (following numbers) approximately ◊ (verb suffix) ◊ Lai (surname)

没 méi ◊ not exist, not have, not be there, be without ◊ there is not ◊ not as... as ◊ not... than ◊ scarcely less than ◊ not yet ◊ did not ‖ (used like méiyǒu 沒有/没有)

系 xì ◊ system, series, line ◊ department, faculty (at college, university)

识 shí ◊ know, recognize, understand ◊ knowledge, experience

这 zhè ◊ this, these (mostly preceding a measure word or number)

里 lǐ ◊ in, inside (as a postposition)

饭 fàn ◊ meal (usu. with rice); cooked cereals (mostly rice) ◊ {figurative} means of livelihood; living

些 xiē ◊ few, several, some (unspecified amount) ◊ somewhat, slightly ◊ (as a postposition, used to indicate plurality) ◊ {measure word} (used for an indefinite number of people or things, can only be preceded by the numeral yī 一 "one")

京 jīng ◊ (national) capital ◊ (jīng) Beijing ◊ ten million ◊ high hill ◊ vast, great ◊ Jing (surname)

呢 ne ◊ is it so? isn't it? how about...? and...? (question particle used at the end of a question) ◊ surely, certainly (sentence-final particle giving emphasis to a statement) ◊ -ing (at the end of a statement expresses that the action is continuing) ◊ well,... ◊ but (on the other hand)...(interjection used to pause a sentence, often to indicate a contrast)

和 hé ◊ and; with ◊ together with ◊ kind, gentle, mild; (be) on good terms with, harmonious; harmony, peace ◊ {sports} (of the result of a competition) a draw, a tie ◊ Japan, Japanese ◊ He (surname)

国 guó ◊ nation, country, state ◊ national, representing the state ◊ Chinese, of China ◊ the best in the country ◊ {archaic} fiefdom ◊ region (of a country) ◊ capital (city) ◊ Guo (surname)

姐 jiě ◊ elder sister

学 xué ◊ learn, study ◊ imitate, copy, mimic ◊ scholarship, learning, education, study, knowledge, science ◊ subject (of study), (academic) discipline, branch of learning ◊ school, college

店 diàn ◊ shop, store; inn, hotel

明 míng ◊ bright, clear, evident ◊ open, overt ◊ tomorrow; next (year) ◊ know, understand ◊ Ming (dynasty, 1368-1644) ◊ Ming (surname)

朋 péng ◊ friend ◊ form a party, clique, etc. ◊ in groups ◊ together ◊ rival, equal ◊ peng (form of currency) ◊ Peng (surname)

服 fú ◊ clothing, garments ◊ wear, put on (clothes) ◊ take (medicine) ◊ assume (a post), serve (in the military, a prison sentence, etc.) ◊ submit oneself to, obey ◊ cause to accept, convince ◊ be used to, accustomed to ◊ Fu (surname)

杯 bēi ◊ (variant of 杯) cup, glass; cup (as a trophy) ◊ {measure word}... cup(s) of...,... glass(es) of...(used for the quantity of liquid which a cup or glass can hold)
果 guǒ ◊ fruit(s); nuts ◊ result, effect, consequence, outcome ◊ decisive, resolute, strong-willed, determined ◊ as expected, really ◊ if indeed ◊ Guo (surname)
爸 bà ◊ {colloquial} dad, pa, father, daddy
狗 gǒu ◊ dog, Canis lupus familiaris ◊ {abusive} damned (person, etc.); lackey
现 xiàn ◊ appear, become visible/manifest, manifest (itself), be revealed ◊ present, current, concrete; now ◊ at the time, extemporaneous ◊ ready, on hand (like cash)
的 de ◊ {grammar} (as an attributive suffix) "of a certain quality" (like xīn de fángzi 新的房子 "a new house") ◊ (as a possessive suffix) "of" (like tā de zìxíngchē 他的自行車/他的自行车 "his bicycle") ◊ (as a noun-forming suffix) "the... ones" (like yǒu niánqīng de, yǒu lǎo de 有年輕的,有老的/有年轻的,有老的 "there were young ones and old ones")
苹 píng ◊ apple, Malas pumila
视 shì ◊ look at, view, examine ◊ regard, consider, treat as, look upon as ◊ inspect, observe, watch, contrast, compare ◊ model oneself on, follow the example of ◊ {physics} apparent
话 huà ◊ words, talk (spoken or written) ◊ talk about, discuss ◊ speech, language ◊ tell, instruct
雨 yǔ ◊ rain
亮 liàng ◊ bright, luminous, light shine ◊ shining ◊ resonant, sonorous ◊ enlighten, be instructive ◊ show, manifest ◊ transparent
前 qián ◊ in front ◊ forward, ahead ◊ front, first ◊ before, ago ◊ previous, preceding ◊ {Chinese chess} at the front (the piece at the front, relative to the player)
哪 nǎ ◊ (as interrogative particle, mostly followed by a number or measure word) which (one)? what? any ◊ (as a rhetorical question particle) how can...! how could...!
客 kè ◊ guest, visitor ◊ traveler, passenger ◊ stranger ◊ {history} retainer (at a feudal court during the Zhou Dynasty) ◊ itinerant retainer (seeking status as political advisor) ◊ Ke (surname) ◊ {regional, measure word} (of food or drinks in a restaurant, etc.) an order
很 hěn ◊ very, quite (often used as a rhetorical prefix to an adjective, with little or no intensification of the adjective's meaning)
怎 zěn ◊ why, how
星 xīng ◊ {astronomy} star ◊ heavenly body (which emits or reflects light) ◊ bit, particle ◊ Xing (one of the 28 Lunar Mansions) ◊ xing (musical instrument of two small copper cymbals) ◊ Xing (surname)
昨 zuó ◊ yesterday ◊ in the past, formerly
是 shì ◊ be, am, is, are (equating two things) ◊ right ◊ yes (response when called on) ◊ {classical} this ◊ {classical} correct, right ◊ (in the pattern 是...是...) is it...or is it...? ◊ "Yes!" ◊ "Right!"
点 diǎn ◊ point, dot, spot, stain ◊ drop (of a liquid) ◊ {math} (decimal) point ◊ {measure word} a little (of sth), some, a bit of... ◊ {measure word} point (also used for counting abstract items like proposals, comments, reasons) ◊ incline one's head, nod ◊ drip, administer in drops ◊ stain, tarnish ◊ {agriculture} dibble, plant in holes ◊ hint, point out, indicate ◊ ignite, light, kindle ◊ adorn, embellish ◊ choose, order (like a dish) ◊ point, spot (location) ◊ selected spots (in contrast to miàn 面 "the whole area") ◊ metal bell or clapper to announce the hour; hour, o'clock ◊ {grammar} (a bit) more... (shortened form of 一点 used after an adjective, e.g., kuài diǎn 快點/快点 "faster") ◊ cakes, refreshments, snacks ◊ {printing} point (size of type, approx. 3.5 mm) ◊ point to ◊

touch lightly and very briefly ◊ {IT} click (=diǎnjī 點擊/点击)
看 kàn ◊ look, see, read ◊ think, view (the situation) ◊ visit, call on (friends, etc.)
茶 chá ◊ tea (leaves); tea (the beverage) ◊ certain kinds of beverages ◊ tea oil ◊ dark brown ◊ {archaic} betrothal gift ◊ {archaic, formal} a young girl (Táng 唐 Dynasty term)
觉 jué ◊ feel, think, sense ◊ sensation, perception ◊ wake up, awake ◊ become awakened, come to realize, find out, discover, become aware (of), become conscious (of)
语 yǔ ◊ language, words ◊ speak, say ◊ saying, idiom ◊ signal, sign (language)
说 shuō ◊ speak, say, talk ◊ explain, give an explanation ◊ theory, doctrine, views ◊ scold, criticize ◊ act as go-between or matchmaker, introduce ◊ refer to, hint, indicate ◊ point to
钟 zhōng ◊ bell (as a musical instrument) ◊ clock (like alarm clock, wall clock) ◊ hour, minute
院 yuàn ◊ courtyard, yard ◊ (character used to designate various government or public buildings) college, academy, institute, school ◊ branch of the government (like the Lìfǎyuàn 立法院 "Legislative Commission" of Taiwan)
面 miàn ◊ face (toward); face, surface ◊ aspect ◊ the whole area (in contrast to diǎn 點/点 "selected spots") ◊ {regional, slang} habitually slow (of a person) ◊ {measure word} (used for things with a flat surface, like walls, mirrors, etc.)
候 hòu ◊ wait, await, expect ◊ visit, inquire after ◊ {dialect} treat, pick up the cheque ◊ time, period, season ◊ (of an ongoing process, or a situation in flux) condition, state ◊ {Chinese calendar} pentad (a period of five days, three of which constitute a jiéqì 節氣/节气 "solar term") ◊ {admin, archaic} official in charge of protocol ◊ {archaic} frontier lookout post
家 jiā ◊ family, household; home, residence ◊ (as suffix) expert/specialist in a certain field (like zuòjiā 作家 "writer") ◊ {philosophy} school (of thought) (like rújiā 儒家 "the Confucian school") ◊ party, side ◊ {humble} my... ◊ {regional} (of animals) tamed, broken, domesticated ◊ {measure word} (used for families, companies, hotels, stores, etc.) ◊ Jia (surname)
校 xiào ◊ school ◊ {military} military camp; field officer ◊ Xiao (surname)
样 yàng ◊ appearance, shape, form ◊ model, sample, pattern ◊ {measure word} (for kind or type of thing)
桌 zhuō ◊ table, desk ◊ {measure word}... tableful(s) of... (used for tables with dishes and wine, and for people seated at a table)
热 rè ◊ hot ◊ ardent, fervent ◊ crave, be envious ◊ popular, in demand ◊ fad, craze, rage ◊ thermal ◊ {med} hot (one of the Eight Principal Syndromes, see Bā Gāng 八綱/八纲)
爱 ài ◊ love, like, be fond of... ◊ have deep affection for... ◊ cherish, treasure, hold dear ◊ have the habit of doing sth, like to do sth, be apt to do sth ◊ Ai (surname) ◊ whether or not (used with bù 不 "not" in front of the same verb to indicate free choice, e.g., àixìn-bùxìn 愛信不信/爱信不信 "believe it or not", or àiyào-bùyào 愛要不要/爱要不要 "take it or leave it")
租 zū ◊ rent, hire ◊ rent out, lease out ◊ rent ◊ land tax
站 zhàn ◊ stand, take a stand ◊ stop, cease; a stop, station ◊ service centre, service station ◊ {measure word}... stop(s) of... (used for the stops of a train/bus) ◊ {IT} (short for wǎngzhàn 網站/网站) website
能 néng ◊ can ◊ be possible ◊ capable ◊ energy (such as in yuánzǐnéng 原子能 "atomic energy")
脑 nǎo ◊ brain ◊ {figurative} brains, head ◊ extract, essence
请 qǐng ◊ request, ask ◊ please ◊ invite; treat (sb to dinner, etc.) ◊ engage, hire, retain (a teacher, nurse, lawyer, fengshui consultant, etc.); send

for (a doctor, etc.) ◊ {archaic} buy (incense, candles, and various other accessories for religious worship) ◊ call on, pay one's respects

读 dú ◊ read aloud ◊ read ◊ study (a subject in school), attend (school)

谁 shéi ◊ who? ◊ anyone

起 qǐ ◊ rise, stand up ◊ (as a verb suffix) begin to..., start to... ◊ give rise to (e.g., change) ◊ exert (e.g., influence) ◊ give (a name) ◊ {measure word}... case(s) of...,... instance(s) of... (used for criminal cases, lawsuits, disputes, fires, accidents, murders, burglaries, etc.)

都 dōu ◊ all, both, every, in every case ◊ (when preceding shì 是, indicates the cause of sth that happened) it's all because of... ◊ (following a stressed subject, or in the pattern lián 連/连 ... dōu 都 ...) even..., already... (as in Dōu shíyī diǎn le! 都十一點了/都十一点了！"It's eleven o'clock already!") ◊ (used in a question with an interrogative pronoun to ask for a plural answer, e.g., Nǐ dōu mǎi shénme le 你都買甚麼了/你都买什么了？ "What things did you buy?")

钱 qián ◊ money; cash ◊ coin ◊ {unit of weight} qian (approx. equivalent to 5 grams) ◊ Qian (surname)

高 gāo ◊ high, tall (in contrast to dī 低 "low"); height ◊ (of quality, etc.) above average, top, superior, advanced ◊ of high(er) rank/degree/level ◊ (of sound) (too) loud/sharp/high ◊ {honorific} your, his/her, their (opinion, etc.) ◊ old, aged ◊ expensive, dear ◊ {colloquial, new usage} tipsy/drunk, "high" (on alcohol or drugs) (a literal translation of English "high") ◊ {chem} (of a chemical compound) "high-oxygen"; containing one more oxygen atom (as in gāoměngsuānjiǎ 高錳酸鉀/高锰酸钾 "potassium permanganate") ◊ {math, geometry} the altitude (like of a triangle) ◊ Gao (surname)

做 zuò ◊ work, do ◊ make, create, manufacture, produce ◊ be, become, act as, be used as ◊ write, compose ◊ play the part of, disguise oneself as ◊ hold (a celebration, like a birthday)

商 shāng ◊ confer, consult, discuss ◊ commerce, business, trade ◊ commercial ◊ merchant, businessman, trader ◊ profiteer ◊ {math} quotient ◊ [Sh-] Shang Dynasty (16th-11th century BCE) ◊ Shang (surname)

猫 māo ◊ cat (domestic cat, house cat, Felis silvestris catus) ◊ {dialect} hide, go into hiding

菜 cài ◊ vegetables, greens ◊ canola, rapeseed (oil) ◊ dish, course (of a meal, on a menu, etc.) ◊ meal, dishes; food

馆 guǎn ◊ guesthouse, hotel ◊ embassy, consulate ◊ shop, place of business (like a restaurant) ◊ library, museum, exhibition hall, gymnasium (and other buildings serving cultural/sports activities) ◊ {archaic} old-style private school

喂 wèi ◊ hello (or other interjection to attract sb's attention)

喜 xǐ ◊ be happy, be delighted ◊ happy event ◊ blessed event, pregnancy ◊ like, be fond of ◊ Xi (surname)

喝 hē ◊ drink ◊ drink alcoholic beverages

期 qī ◊ term, period of time ◊ phase/stage (of a project) ◊ scheduled time, set time ◊ {measure word}... issue(s) of...,... class(es) of... (used for things produced periodically, like issues of a magazine/newspaper, and for classes of students) ◊ set up/schedule (an appointment, etc.) ◊ expect, await, hope (for), anticipate, look forward to ◊ Qi (surname)

椅 yǐ ◊ chair

谢 xiè ◊ thank ◊ apologize ◊ decline (an invitation, etc.) ◊ take one's leave ◊ fall (of leaves, flowers) ◊ wither and fall ◊ die of old age ◊ Xie (city in Tanghe, Hénán 河南 Province) ◊ Xie (surname)

想 xiǎng ◊ think (of); intend; be keen on sth ◊ want to, would like to ◊ long for, recall with fondness, miss, think of ◊ desire

睡 shuì ◊ sleep, go to sleep, fall asleep

零 líng ◊ zero, 0, nought, nil ◊ fragments, remnants ◊ fragmentary, fractional ◊ odd (number, amount, etc.) ◊ (on a thermometer) zero (degrees) ◊ (of leaves, etc.) wither and fall ◊ light rain ◊ Ling (surname)

漂 piāo ◊ float, drift ◊ stay afloat ◊ shake, rock ◊ (of wind) blow

影 yǐng ◊ shadow, image ◊ trace, sign ◊ reflection ◊ photograph ◊ motion picture, movie ◊ video ◊ portrait of an ancestor ◊ shadow play ◊ hide, conceal ◊ sundial

HSK Level 1
Chinese Character Stroke Order

字	部首	Definition and Stroke
一 yī	一	①one ②1 ③single ④a (article) ⑤as soon as ⑥entire ⑦whole ⑧all ⑨throughout ⑩"one" radical in Chinese characters (Kangxi radical 1)
七 qī	一	①seven ②7
九 jiǔ	乙	①nine ②9
了 le	亅	①to finish ②to achieve ③to understand ④(modal particle intensifying preceding clause) ⑤(completed action marker) ⑥(of eyes) bright ⑦clear-sighted ⑧to understand clearly ⑨to watch from a height or distance ⑩to survey ⑪(of eyes) bright ⑫clear-sighted ⑬to understand clearly ⑭to watch from a height or distance ⑮to survey
二 èr	二	①two ②2 ③stupid (Beijing dialect)
人 rén	人〔亻〕	①man ②person ③people ④CL:個|个[gè],位[wèi]
儿 r·	儿〔兀〕	①non-syllabic diminutive suffix ②retroflex final ③son ④non-syllabic diminutive suffix ⑤retroflex final ⑥son
八 bā	八	①eight ②8
几 jǐ	几	①small table ②how much ③how many ④several ⑤a few ⑥almost ⑦how much ⑧how many ⑨several ⑩a few ⑪almost
十 shí	十	①ten ②10

HSK Level 1
Chinese Character Stroke Order

字	部首	Definition and Stroke
三 sān	一	①three ②3 ③surname San
上 shàng	一	①on top ②upon ③above ④upper ⑤previous ⑥first (of multiple parts) ⑦to climb ⑧to get onto ⑨to go up ⑩to attend (class or university) ⑪see 上聲|上声[shǎng shēng]
下 xià	一	①down ②downwards ③below ④lower ⑤later ⑥next (week etc) ⑦second (of two parts) ⑧to decline ⑨to go down ⑩to arrive at (a decision, conclusion etc)
个 gè	丨	①individual ②this ③that ④size ⑤classifier for people or objects in general
么 yāo	丿	①youngest ②most junior ③tiny ④one (unambiguous spoken form when spelling out numbers, esp. on telephone or in military) ⑤one or ace on dice or dominoes ⑥variant of 幺, to shout ⑦suffix, used to form interrogative 基麼|什么, what?, indefinite 這麼|这么 thus etc ⑧tiny ⑨insignificant ⑩exclamatory final particle ⑪interrogative final particle ⑫variant of 麼|么 ⑬suffix, used to form interrogative 基麼|什么, what?, indefinite 這麼|这么 thus etc ⑭tiny ⑮insignificant ⑯exclamatory final particle ⑰interrogative final particle ⑱one ⑲one on dice ⑳tiny ㉑small ㉒insignificant ㉓the youngest son or daughter of a family ㉔lone ㉕alone ㉖a Chinese family name ㉗variant of 麼|么
习 xí	冫	①to practice ②to study ③habit ④surname Xi
大 dà	大	①big ②huge ③large ④major ⑤great ⑥wide ⑦deep ⑧oldest ⑨eldest ⑩see 大夫[dài fu]
女 nǚ	女	①female ②woman ③daughter ④archaic variant of 汝[rǔ]
子 zi	子	①(noun suffix) ②son ③child ④seed ⑤egg ⑥small thing ⑦1st earthly branch: 11 p.m.-1 a.m., midnight, 11th solar month (7th December to 5th January), year of the Rat ⑧Viscount, fourth of five orders of nobility 五等爵位[wǔ děng jué wèi]
小 xiǎo	小[⺌]	①small ②tiny ③few ④young

HSK Level 1
Chinese Character Stroke Order

字	部首	Definition and Stroke
工 gōng	工	①work ②worker ③skill ④profession ⑤trade ⑥craft ⑦labor
飞 fēi	乙	①to fly
不 bù	一	①(negative prefix) ②not ③no
中 zhōng	丨	①within ②among ③in ④middle ⑤center ⑥while (doing sth) ⑦during ⑧China ⑨Chinese ⑩surname Zhong ⑪to hit (the mark) ⑫to be hit by ⑬to suffer ⑭to win (a prize, a lottery)
书 shū	丨	①book ②letter ③document ④CL:本[běn],册丨册[cè],部[bù] ⑤to write ⑥abbr. for 書經丨书经[shū jīng]
五 wǔ	二	①five ②5
什 shí	人[亻]	①ten (used in fractions, writing checks etc) ②assorted ③miscellaneous
今 jīn	人[亻]	①today ②modern ③present ④current ⑤this ⑥now
六 liù	八	①six ②6
分 fēn	刀[刂]	①to divide ②to separate ③to distribute ④to allocate ⑤to distinguish (good and bad) ⑥part or subdivision ⑦fraction ⑧one tenth (of certain units) ⑨unit of length equivalent to 0.33 cm ⑩minute ⑪a point (in sports or games) ⑫0.01 yuan (unit of money) ⑬part ⑭share ⑮ingredient ⑯component

HSK Level 1
Chinese Character Stroke Order

字	部首	Definition and Stroke
午 wǔ	十	①7th earthly branch: 11 a.m.-1 p.m., noon, 5th solar month (6th June-6th July), year of the Horse
友 yǒu	又	①friend
天 tiān	大	①day ②sky ③heaven
太 tài	大	①highest ②greatest ③too (much) ④very ⑤extremely
少 shǎo	小[⺌]	①few ②little ③lack ④young
开 kāi	廾	①to open ②to start ③to turn on ④to boil ⑤to write out (a prescription, check, invoice etc) ⑥to operate (vehicle) ⑦abbr. for 開爾文|开尔文 degrees Kelvin
日 rì	日	①sun ②day ③date, day of the month ④abbr. for 日本 Japan
月 yuè	月	①moon ②month ③CL:個|个[gè],輪|轮[lún]
气 qì	气	①gas ②air ③smell ④weather ⑤to make angry ⑥to annoy ⑦to get angry ⑧vital energy ⑨qi ⑩gas ⑪air ⑫smell ⑬weather ⑭to make angry ⑮to annoy ⑯to get angry ⑰vital energy ⑱qi
水 shuǐ	水[氵]	①water ②river ③liquid ④beverage ⑤additional charges or income ⑥(of clothes) classifier for number of washes ⑦surname Shui

HSK Level 1
Chinese Character Stroke Order

字	部首	Definition and Stroke
火 huǒ	火[灬]	①fire ②urgent ③ammunition ④fiery or flaming ⑤internal heat (Chinese medicine) ⑥hot (popular) ⑦classifier for military units (old) ⑧surname Huo 火 火 火 火
见 jiàn	见	①to see ②to meet ③to appear (to be sth) ④to interview ⑤to appear 见 见 见 见
认 rèn	讠	①to recognize ②to know ③to admit 认 认 认 认
车 chē	车	①car ②vehicle ③CL:辆丨辆[liàng] ④machine ⑤to shape with a lathe ⑥surname Che ⑦war chariot (archaic) ⑧rook (in Chinese chess) ⑨rook (in chess) 车 车 车 车
东 dōng	一	①east ②host (i.e. sitting on east side of guest) ③landlord ④surname Dong 东 东 东 东 东
他 tā	人[亻]	①he or him ②(used for either sex when the sex is unknown or unimportant) ③(used before sb's name for emphasis) ④(used as a meaningless mock object) ⑤other ⑥another 他 他 他 他 他
们 men	人[亻]	①plural marker for pronouns, and nouns referring to individuals 们 们 们 们 们
写 xiě	冖	①to write 写 写 写 写 写
出 chū	凵	①to go out ②to come out ③to occur ④to produce ⑤to go beyond ⑥to rise ⑦to put forth ⑧to happen ⑨classifier for dramas, plays, operas etc 出 出 出 出 出
北 běi	匕	①north ②to be defeated (classical) 北 北 北 北 北

HSK Level 1
Chinese Character Stroke Order

字	部首	Definition and Stroke
去 qù	厶	①to go ②to go to (a place) ③to cause to go or send (sb) ④to remove ⑤to get rid of ⑥(when used either before or after a verb) to go in order to do sth ⑦to be apart from in space or time ⑧(after a verb of motion indicates movement away from the speaker) ⑨(used after certain verbs to indicate detachment or separation) ⑩(of a time or an event etc) just passed or elapsed 去 去 去 去 去
叫 jiào	口	①to shout ②to call ③to order ④to ask ⑤to be called ⑥by (indicates agent in the passive mood) 叫 叫 叫 叫 叫
四 sì	口	①four ②4 四 四 四 四 四
对 duì	寸	①couple ②pair ③to be opposite ④to oppose ⑤to face ⑥versus ⑦for ⑧to ⑨correct (answer) ⑩to answer ⑪to reply ⑫to direct (towards sth) ⑬right 对 对 对 对 对
打 dǎ	手[扌]	①to beat ②to strike ③to hit ④to break ⑤to type ⑥to mix up ⑦to build ⑧to fight ⑨to fetch ⑩to make ⑪to tie up ⑫to issue ⑬to shoot ⑭to calculate ⑮to play (a game) ⑯since ⑰from ⑱dozen 打 打 打 打 打
本 běn	木	①roots or stems of plants ②origin ③source ④this ⑤the current ⑥root ⑦foundation ⑧basis ⑨classifier for books, periodicals, files etc ⑩originally 本 本 本 本 本
汉 hàn	水[氵]	①Han ethnic group ②Chinese (language) ③the Han dynasty (206 BC-220 AD) ④man 汉 汉 汉 汉 汉
生 shēng	生	①to be born ②to give birth ③life ④to grow ⑤raw, uncooked 生 生 生 生 生
电 diàn	日	①electric ②electricity ③electrical 电 电 电 电 电
买 mǎi	大	①to buy ②to purchase 买 买 买 买 买 买

HSK Level 1
Chinese Character Stroke Order

字	部首	Definition and Stroke
会 huì	人[亻]	①can ②be possible ③be able to ④will ⑤be likely to ⑥be sure to ⑦to assemble ⑧to meet ⑨to gather ⑩to see ⑪union ⑫group ⑬association ⑭CL:個|个[gè] ⑮a moment (Taiwan pr. for this sense is [huǐ]) ⑯to balance an account ⑰accountancy ⑱accounting
先 xiān	儿[兀]	①early ②prior ③former ④in advance ⑤first
关 guān	八	①mountain pass ②to close ③to shut ④to turn off ⑤to concern ⑥to involve ⑦surname Guan
兴 xīng	八	①to rise ②to flourish ③to become popular ④to start ⑤to encourage ⑥to get up ⑦(often used in the negative) to permit or allow (topolect) ⑧maybe (topolect) ⑨surname Xing ⑩feeling or desire to do sth ⑪interest in sth ⑫excitement
再 zài	冂	①again ②once more ③re- ④second ⑤another ⑥then (after sth, and not until then)
吃 chī	口	①to eat ②to consume ③to eat at (a cafeteria etc) ④to eradicate ⑤to destroy ⑥to absorb ⑦to suffer
同 tóng	口	①like ②same ③similar ④together ⑤alike ⑥with ⑦see 衚衕|胡同[hú tòng] ⑧see 衚衕|胡同[hú tòng]
名 míng	口	①name ②noun (part of speech) ③place (e.g. among winners) ④famous ⑤classifier for people
后 hòu	口	①empress ②queen ③surname Hou ④back ⑤behind ⑥rear ⑦afterwards ⑧after ⑨later ⑩back ⑪behind ⑫rear ⑬afterwards ⑭after ⑮later
吗 ma	口	①see 嗎啡|吗啡, morphine ②(question tag)

HSK Level 1
Chinese Character Stroke Order

字	部首	Definition and Stroke
回 huí	口	①to circle ②to go back ③to turn around ④to answer ⑤to return ⑥to revolve ⑦Hui ethnic group (Chinese Muslims) ⑧time ⑨classifier for acts of a play ⑩section or chapter (of a classic book)
在 zài	土	①(located) at ②(to be) in ③to exist ④in the middle of doing sth ⑤(indicating an action in progress)
多 duō	夕	①many ②much ③a lot of ④numerous ⑤more ⑥in excess ⑦how (to what extent) ⑧multi- ⑨Taiwan pr. [duó] when it means "how"
她 tā	女	①she
好 hǎo	女	①good ②well ③proper ④good to ⑤easy to ⑥very ⑦so ⑧(suffix indicating completion or readiness) ⑨to be in love (e.g. 学姐，你跟他好了，就不怕代沟么？) ⑩to be fond of ⑪to have a tendency to ⑫to be prone to
妈 mā	女	①ma ②mom ③mother
字 zì	子	①letter ②symbol ③character ④word ⑤CL:個|个[gè] ⑥courtesy or style name traditionally given to males aged 20 in dynastic China
岁 suì	山	①classifier for years (of age) ②year ③year (of crop harvests)
师 shī	巾	①teacher ②master ③expert ④model ⑤army division ⑥(old) troops ⑦to dispatch troops ⑧surname Shi
年 nián	干	①year ②CL:個|个[gè] ③surname Nian

HSK Level 1
Chinese Character Stroke Order

字	部首	Definition and Stroke
有 yǒu	月	①to have ②there is ③there are ④to exist ⑤to be
机 jī	木	①machine ②engine ③opportunity ④intention ⑤aircraft ⑥pivot ⑦crucial point ⑧flexible (quick-witted) ⑨organic ⑩CL:臺|台[tái] ⑪surname Ji ⑫machine ⑬engine ⑭opportunity ⑮intention ⑯aircraft ⑰pivot ⑱crucial point ⑲flexible (quick-witted) ⑳organic ㉑CL:臺|台[tái] ㉒surname Ji
欢 huān	欠	①joyous ②happy ③pleased
米 mǐ	米	①rice ②CL:粒[lì] ③meter (classifier) ④surname Mi
老 lǎo	老	①prefix used before the surname of a person or a numeral indicating the order of birth of the children in a family or to indicate affection or familiarity ②old (of people) ③venerable (person) ④experienced ⑤of long standing ⑥always ⑦all the time ⑧of the past ⑨very ⑩outdated ⑪(of meat etc) tough
衣 yī	衣[衤]	①clothes ②CL:件[jiàn] ③to dress ④to wear ⑤to put on (clothes)
西 xī	西	①west ②the West ③abbr. for Spain 西班牙[Xī bān yá] ④Spanish
那 nà	邑[阝右]	①that ②those ③then (in that case) ④commonly pr. [nèi] before a classifier, esp. in Beijing ⑤variant of 哪[nǎ]
住 zhù	人[亻]	①to live ②to dwell ③to stay ④to reside ⑤to stop ⑥(suffix indicating firmness, steadiness, or coming to a halt)
作 zuò	人[亻]	①to do ②to grow ③to write or compose ④to pretend ⑤to regard as ⑥to feel ⑦writings or works

HSK Level 1
Chinese Character Stroke Order

字	部首	Definition and Stroke
你 nǐ	人[亻]	①you (informal, as opposed to courteous 您[nín])
冷 lěng	冫	①cold ②surname Leng
医 yī	匚	①medical ②medicine ③doctor ④to cure ⑤to treat
听 tīng	口	①to listen ②to hear ③to obey ④a can (loanword from English "tin") ⑤classifier for canned beverages ⑥(literary pronunciation, still advocated in Taiwan) to rule ⑦to sentence ⑧to allow
坐 zuò	土	①to sit ②to take a seat ③to take (a bus, airplane etc) ④to bear fruit ⑤variant of 座 [zuò]
块 kuài	土	①lump (of earth) ②chunk ③piece ④classifier for pieces of cloth, cake, soap etc ⑤colloquial word for yuan (or other unit of currency such as Hong Kong or US dollar etc), usually as 塊錢|块钱
我 wǒ	戈	①I ②me ③my
时 shí	日	①o'clock ②time ③when ④hour ⑤season ⑥period ⑦surname Shi
来 lái	木	①to come ②to arrive ③to come round ④ever since ⑤next
没 méi	水[氵]	①(negative prefix for verbs) ②have not ③not ④drowned ⑤to end ⑥to die ⑦to inundate

HSK Level 1
Chinese Character Stroke Order

字	部首	Definition and Stroke
系 xì	系	①system ②department ③faculty ④to connect ⑤to relate to ⑥to tie up ⑦to bind ⑧to be (literary) ⑨to connect ⑩to arrest ⑪to worry ⑫to tie ⑬to fasten ⑭to button up ⑮to connect ⑯to relate to ⑰to tie up ⑱to bind ⑲to be (literary) ⑳to connect ㉑to arrest ㉒to worry ㉓to tie ㉔to fasten ㉕to button up
识 shí	讠	①to know ②knowledge ③Taiwan pr. [shì] ④to record ⑤to write a footnote
这 zhè	辶[辵]	①this ②these ③(commonly pr. [zhèi] before a classifier, esp. in Beijing)
里 lǐ	里	①li (Chinese mile) ②500 meters (modern) ③home ④hometown ⑤village ⑥neighborhood ⑦administrative unit ⑧Li (surname) ⑨lining interior ⑩inside ⑪internal ⑫also written 裏|里[lǐ] ⑬lining ⑭interior ⑮inside ⑯internal ⑰also written 裏|里[lǐ] ⑱lining ⑲interior ⑳inside ㉑internal ㉒also written 裏|里[lǐ] ㉓lining ㉔interior ㉕inside ㉖internal ㉗also written 裏|里[lǐ]
饭 fàn	饣	①food ②cuisine ③cooked rice ④meal ⑤CL:碗[wǎn],顿|頓[dùn]
些 xiē	二	①some ②few ③several ④measure word indicating a small amount or small number (greater than 1)
京 jīng	亠	①capital city of a country ②big ③algebraic term for a large number (old) ④artificial mound (old) ⑤abbr. for Beijing ⑥surname Jing ⑦Jing ethnic minority
呢 ní	口	①woolen material ②particle indicating that a previously asked question is to be applied to the preceding word ("What about ...?", "And ...?") ③particle for inquiring about location ("Where is ...?") ④particle signaling a pause, to emphasize the preceding words and allow the listener time to take them on board ("ok?", "are you with me?") ⑤(at the end of a declarative sentence) particle indicating continuation of a state or action ⑥particle indicating strong affirmation
和 hé	口	①and ②together with ③with ④sum ⑤union ⑥peace ⑦harmony ⑧Taiwan pr. [hàn] when it means "and" ⑨surname He ⑩Japanese (food, clothes etc) ⑪cap (a poem) ⑫to respond in singing ⑬to mix together ⑭to blend ⑮soft ⑯warm ⑰to complete a set in mahjong or playing cards
国 guó	囗	①country ②nation ③state ④national ⑤CL:个|個[gè] ⑥surname Guo

HSK Level 1
Chinese Character Stroke Order

字	部首	Definition and Stroke
姐 jiě	女	①older sister
学 xué	子	①to learn ②to study ③science ④-ology
店 diàn	广	①inn ②shop ③store ④CL:家[jiā]
明 míng	日	①bright ②opposite: dark 暗[àn] ③(of meaning) clear ④to understand ⑤next ⑥public or open ⑦wise ⑧generic term for a sacrifice to the gods ⑨Ming Dynasty (1368-1644) ⑩surname Ming ⑪Ming (c. 2000 BC), fourth of the legendary Flame Emperors, 炎帝[Yán dì] descended from Shennong 神農|神农[Shén nóng] Farmer God
朋 péng	月	①friend
服 fú	月	①clothes ②dress ③garment ④to serve ⑤to obey ⑥to convince ⑦to acclimatize ⑧to take (medicine) ⑨mourning clothes ⑩to wear mourning clothes ⑪dose (measure word for medicine)
杯 bēi	木	①cup ②classifier for certain containers of liquids: glass, cup
果 guǒ	木	①fruit ②result ③resolute ④indeed ⑤if really
爸 bà	父	①father ②dad ③pa ④papa
狗 gǒu	犬[犭]	①dog ②CL:隻|只[zhī],條|条[tiáo]

HSK Level 1
Chinese Character Stroke Order

字	部首	Definition and Stroke
现 xiàn	玉[王]	①to appear ②present ③now ④existing ⑤current
的 de	白	①of ②~'s (possessive particle) ③(used after an attribute) ④(used to form a nominal expression) ⑤(used at the end of a declarative sentence for emphasis) ⑥aim ⑦clear ⑧really and truly
苹 píng	艸[艹]	①apple ②marsiliaceae ③clover fern
视 shì	见	①to look at ②to regard ③to inspect
话 huà	讠	①dialect ②language ③spoken words ④speech ⑤talk ⑥words ⑦conversation ⑧what sb said ⑨CL:种|种[zhǒng],席[xí],句[jù],口[kǒu],番[fān]
雨 yǔ	雨	①rain ②CL:阵|阵[zhèn],场|场[cháng] ③to rain ④(of rain, snow etc) to fall ⑤to precipitate ⑥to wet
亮 liàng	亠	①bright ②clear ③resonant ④to shine ⑤to show ⑥to reveal
前 qián	刀[刂]	①front ②forward ③ahead ④ago ⑤before ⑥first ⑦former ⑧formerly ⑨future ⑩BC (e.g. 前293年)
哪 nǎ	口	①how ②which ③(particle equivalent to 啊 after noun ending in -n) ④which? (interrogative, followed by classifier or numeral-classifier)
客 kè	宀	①customer ②visitor ③guest

HSK Level 1
Chinese Character Stroke Order

字	部首	Definition and Stroke
很 hěn	彳	①(adverb of degree) ②quite ③very ④awfully
怎 zěn	心[忄]	①how
星 xīng	日	①star ②satellite ③small amount
昨 zuó	日	①yesterday
是 shì	日	①is ②are ③am ④yes ⑤to be
点 diǎn	火[灬]	①point ②dot ③drop ④speck ⑤o'clock ⑥point (in space or time) ⑦to draw a dot ⑧to check on a list ⑨to choose ⑩to order (food in a restaurant) ⑪to touch briefly ⑫to hint ⑬to light ⑭to ignite ⑮to pour a liquid drop by drop ⑯(old) one fifth of a two-hour watch 更[gēng] ⑰dot stroke in Chinese characters ⑱classifier for items
看 kàn	目[罒]	①to see ②to look at ③to read ④to watch ⑤to consider ⑥to regard as ⑦to view as ⑧to treat as ⑨to judge ⑩(after repeated verb) to give it a try ⑪depending on (how you're judging) ⑫to visit ⑬to call on ⑭to treat (an illness) ⑮to look after ⑯Watch out! (for a danger) ⑰to look after ⑱to take care of ⑲to watch ⑳to guard
茶 chá	艸[艹]	①tea ②tea plant ③CL:杯[bēi],壶|壺[hú]
觉 jué	见	①to feel ②to find that ③thinking ④awake ⑤aware ⑥a nap ⑦a sleep ⑧CL:场|場[cháng]
语 yǔ	讠	①dialect ②language ③speech ④to tell to

HSK Level 1
Chinese Character Stroke Order

字	部首	Definition and Stroke
说 shuì	讠	①to speak ②to say ③to explain ④to scold ⑤to tell off ⑥a theory (usually in compounds such as 日心说 heliocentric theory) ⑦to canvass ⑧to persuade ⑨see 遊說/游说[yóu shuì], to canvass and 说客|说客[shuì kè], persuasive speaker ⑩Japanese variant of 說|说 ⑪to speak ⑫to say
钟 zhōng	钅	①clock ②o'clock ③time as measured in hours and minutes ④bell ⑤CL:架[jià],座[zuò] ⑥handleless cup ⑦goblet ⑧to concentrate ⑨variant of 鍾|钟[zhōng] ⑩variant of 鐘|钟 ⑪surname Zhong
院 yuàn	阜[⻖左]	①courtyard ②institution ③CL:个|个[gè]
面 miàn	面	①face ②side ③surface ④aspect ⑤top ⑥classifier for flat surfaces such as drums, mirrors, flags etc ⑦flour ⑧noodles ⑨flour ⑩noodles
候 hòu	人[亻]	①to wait ②to inquire after ③to watch ④season ⑤climate ⑥(old) period of five days
家 jiā	宀	①home ②family ③(polite) my (sister, uncle etc) ④classifier for families or businesses ⑤refers to the philosophical schools of pre-Han China ⑥noun suffix for a specialist in some activity, such as a musician or revolutionary, corresponding to English -ist, -er, -ary or -ian ⑦CL:个|个[gè] ⑧surname Jia
校 xiào	木	①school ②military officer ③CL:所[suǒ] ④to proofread ⑤to check ⑥to compare
样 yàng	木	①manner ②pattern ③way ④appearance ⑤shape ⑥CL:个|个[gè]
桌 zhuō	木	①table
热 rè	火[灬]	①to warm up ②to heat up ③hot (of weather) ④heat ⑤fervent

HSK Level 1
Chinese Character Stroke Order

字	部首	Definition and Stroke
爱 ài	爪[⺥]	①to love ②affection ③to be fond of ④to like
租 zū	禾	①to hire ②to rent ③to charter ④to rent out ⑤to lease out ⑥rent ⑦land tax
站 zhàn	立	①station ②to stand ③to halt ④to stop ⑤branch of a company or organization ⑥website
能 néng	肉[月]	①to be able to ②to be capable of ③ability ④capability ⑤able ⑥capable ⑦can possibly ⑧(usually used in the negative) to have the possibility of ⑨surname Neng
脑 nǎo	肉[月]	①brain ②mind ③head ④essence
请 qǐng	讠	①to ask ②to invite ③please (do sth) ④to treat (to a meal etc) ⑤to request
读 dú	讠	①to read ②to study ③reading of word (i.e. pronunciation), similar to 拼音[pīn yīn] ④comma ⑤phrase marked by pause
谁 shéi	讠	①who ②also pr. [shuí]
起 qǐ	走	①to rise ②to raise ③to get up ④to set out ⑤to start ⑥to appear ⑦to launch ⑧to initiate (action) ⑨to draft ⑩to establish ⑪to get (from a depot or counter) ⑫verb suffix, to start ⑬(before place or time) starting from ⑭classifier for occurrences or unpredictable events: case, instance ⑮classifier for groups: batch, group
都 dū	邑[⻏右]	①capital city ②metropolis ③surname Du ④all ⑤both ⑥entirely ⑦(used for emphasis) even ⑧already ⑨(not) at all

HSK Level 1
Chinese Character Stroke Order

字	部首	Definition and Stroke
钱 qián	钅	①coin ②money ③CL:筆|笔[bǐ] ④unit of weight, one tenth of a tael 兩|两[liǎng] ⑤surname Qian
高 gāo	高	①high ②tall ③above average ④loud ⑤your (honorific) ⑥surname Gao
做 zuò	人[亻]	①to do ②to make ③to produce ④to write ⑤to compose ⑥to act as ⑦to engage in ⑧to hold (a party) ⑨to be ⑩to become ⑪to function (in some capacity) ⑫to serve as ⑬to be used for ⑭to form (a bond or relationship) ⑮to pretend ⑯to feign ⑰to act a part ⑱to put on appearance
商 shāng	口	①commerce ②to consult ③quotient ④2nd note in pentatonic scale ⑤the Shang dynasty, 16th to 11th century BC
猫 māo	犬[犭]	①cat ②CL:隻|只[zhī]
菜 cài	艸[艹]	①dish (type of food) ②vegetables ③vegetable ④cuisine ⑤CL:盤|盘[pán],道[dào]
馆 guǎn	饣	①building ②shop ③term for certain service establishments ④embassy or consulate ⑤schoolroom (old) ⑥CL:家[jiā]
喂 wèi	口	①hey ②to feed (an animal, baby, invalid etc)
喜 xǐ	口	①to be fond of ②to like ③to enjoy ④to be happy ⑤to feel pleased ⑥happiness ⑦delight ⑧glad
喝 hē	口	①to drink ②My goodness! ③to shout loudly

HSK Level 1
Chinese Character Stroke Order

字	部首	Definition and Stroke
期 qī	月	①a period of time ②phase ③stage ④(used for issue of a periodical, courses of study) ⑤time ⑥term ⑦period ⑧to hope ⑨Taiwan pr. [qí]
椅 yǐ	木	①chair
谢 xiè	讠	①to thank ②to apologize ③to wither (of flowers, leaves etc) ④to decline ⑤surname Xie
想 xiǎng	心〔忄〕	①to think ②to believe ③to suppose ④to wish ⑤to want ⑥to miss (feel wistful about the absence of sb or sth)
睡 shuì	目〔䀠〕	①to sleep
零 líng	雨	①zero ②nought ③zero sign ④fractional ⑤fragmentary ⑥odd (of numbers) ⑦(placed between two numbers to indicate a smaller quantity followed by a larger one) ⑧fraction ⑨(in mathematics) remainder (after division) ⑩extra ⑪to wither and fall ⑫to wither
漂 piāo	水〔氵〕	①to float ②to drift ③to bleach ④elegant ⑤polished
影 yǐng	彡	①picture ②image ③film ④movie ⑤photograph ⑥reflection ⑦shadow ⑧trace

汉语水平考试

词汇

Words To Know

Words To Know

A

爱 ài ◊ love, like, be fond of... ◊ have deep affection for... ◊ cherish, treasure, hold dear ◊ have the habit of doing sth, like to do sth, be apt to do sth ◊ Ai (surname) ◊ whether or not (used with bù 不 "not" in front of the same verb to indicate free choice, e.g., àixìn-bùxìn 爱信不信/爱信不信 "believe it or not", or àiyào-bùyào 爱要不要/爱要不要 "take it or leave it")

B

八 bā ◊ eight, 8 (note on pronunciation: when followed by a word in the fourth tone, the reading of bā 八 changes to bá [second tone])
爸爸bàba ◊ dad, daddy, pa
杯子bēizi ◊ cup, glass
北京Běijīng ◊ Beijing (Peking)
本 běn ◊ book ◊ {measure word}... volume(s) of...(used for books, scripts, reels of film, etc.) ◊ root, stem (of a plant) ◊ origin, basis, foundation ◊ {finance} capital, principal ◊ original ◊ one's own, native, home ◊ present, current, this ◊ originally ◊ edition ◊ script (of a play) ◊ memorial to the Emperor
不 bù ◊ not ◊ no
不客气 bùkèqi ◊ blunt, rude ◊ {formal} you're welcome, don't mention it ◊ {formal} please don't bother (as said by a guest) ◊ {formal} please make yourself at home (as said by a host)

C

菜 cài ◊ vegetables, greens ◊ canola, rapeseed (oil) ◊ dish, course (of a meal, on a menu, etc.) ◊ meal, dishes; food

茶 chá ◊ tea (leaves); tea (the beverage) ◊ certain kinds of beverages ◊ tea oil ◊ dark brown ◊ {archaic} betrothal gift ◊ {archaic, formal} a young girl (Táng 唐 Dynasty term)

吃 chī ◊ eat, take/have a meal, dine ◊ live on, live off, scrounge off ◊ soak up, absorb, take in ◊ wipe out, annihilate, eat up ◊ understand, grasp ◊ suffer, incur, endure, bear, withstand ◊ consume, exhaust (like one's energy) ◊ {grammar} by (particle indicating the passive voice)

出租车 chūzūchē ◊ taxicab

D

打 dǎ ◊ strike, hit, beat ◊ break, smash, wreck ◊ batter, attack, fight ◊ come into contact with, deal with (as in dǎ jiāodao 打交道 "have dealings with") ◊ build, construct ◊ forge (like a knife) ◊ pack (like luggage) ◊ apply (like paint) ◊ make (like a phone call) ◊ remove (as in the medical term dǎchóng 打蟲/打虫 "deworm") ◊ knit, weave ◊ take/board (a train, plane) ◊ take/get/hire (a taxi) ◊ ladle, fetch (like porridge, water) ◊ hunt/catch (as in dǎyú 打魚/打鱼 "catch fish") ◊ shoot (with a fire-arm) ◊ collect, gather (like firewood) ◊ draft (a document, estimate, etc.) ◊ do (like odd jobs) ◊ label as, charge with ◊ fight (a war, battle) ◊ play (a game, sport) ◊ buy ◊ be about, concern ◊ {colloquial} (used like cóng 從/从) from; (used like cóng 從/从... qǐ 起) beginning at...

电话 diànhuà ◊ telephone ◊ telephone call

大 dà ◊ big, large, great ◊ greatly, to a large extent, in a major way ◊ major, important, main ◊ general ◊ strong, heavy ◊ loud, high (like volume of sound, or sb's voice) ◊ (of persons) old (i.e. of a certain age) ◊ the oldest (among two or more) ◊ adult, elder ◊ (as emphatic prefix) even on...(followed by a time expression, as in dà Xīngqīrì 大星期日 "even on Sundays") ◊ (as honorific prefix) your... ◊ (used for transcription of the syllable -da- in foreign names) ◊ Da (surname)

的 de ◊ {grammar} (as an attributive suffix) "of a certain quality" (like xīn de fángzi 新的房子 "a new house") ◊ (as a possessive suffix) "of" (like tā de zìxíngchē 他的自行車/他的自行车 "his bicycle") ◊ (as a noun-forming suffix) "the... ones" (like yǒu niánqīng de, yǒu lǎo de 有年輕的,有老的/有年轻的,有老的 "there were young ones and old ones")

点 diǎn ◊ point, dot, spot, stain ◊ drop (of a liquid) ◊ {math} (decimal) point ◊ {measure word} a little (of sth), some, a bit of... ◊ {measure word} point (also used for counting abstract items like proposals, comments, reasons) ◊ incline one's head, nod ◊ drip, administer in drops ◊ stain, tarnish ◊ {agriculture} dibble, plant in holes ◊ hint, point out, indicate ◊ ignite, light, kindle ◊ adorn, embellish ◊ choose, order (like a dish) ◊ point, spot (location) ◊ selected spots (in contrast to miàn 面 "the whole area") ◊ metal bell or clapper to announce the hour; hour, o'clock ◊ {grammar} (a bit) more... (shortened form of 一点 used after an adjective, e.g., kuài diǎn 快點/快点 "faster") ◊ cakes, refreshments, snacks ◊ {printing} point (size of type, approx. 3.5 mm) ◊ point to ◊ touch lightly and very briefly ◊ {IT} click (=diǎnjī 點擊/点击)

电脑 diànnǎo ◊ computer ‖ (The formal mainland China word is diànzǐ jìsuànjī 電子計算機/电子计算机)

电视 diànshì ◊ television, TV

电影 diànyǐng ◊ movie, motion picture

东西 dōngxi ◊ thing ◊ creature (used to express dislike of a person or thing)

都 dōu ◊ all, both, every, in every case ◊ (when preceding shì 是, indicates the cause of sth that happened) it's all because of... ◊ (following a stressed subject, or in the pattern lián 連/连 ... dōu 都 ...) even..., already... (as in Dōu shíyī diǎn le! 都十一點了/都十一点了! "It's eleven o'clock already!") ◊ (used in a question with an interrogative pronoun to ask for a plural answer, e.g., Nǐ dōu mǎi shénme le 你都買甚麼了/你都买什么了? "What things did you buy?")

读 dú ◊ read aloud ◊ read ◊ study (a subject in school), attend (school)

对不起 duìbuqǐ ◊ {formal} excuse me, I'm sorry, pardon me ◊ disappoint, do a disservice to ◊ let (sb) down

多 duō ◊ many, much; more, further; in excess, extra, exceeding (the intended/normal/original number or amount) ◊ a lot, ample ◊ (following a numeral) more than..., over (the number/amount stated) ◊ far more, much more ◊ mostly, for the most part ◊ (in questions asking about number, size, etc.) how (much, big, etc.)? ◊ (in exclamations) how...! ◊ Duo (surname)

多少 duōshao ◊ how many; how much ◊ (phrase used to indicate a great or infinite amount; phrase used in the negative to indicate a small amount; phrase used in exclamatory sentences) ◊ (in the pronunciation "duōshǎo") number, amount ◊ more or less

E

儿子 érzi ◊ son
二 èr ◊ two, 2; second; double; dual; binary ◊ second in charge/command, etc., sub-, vice- ◊ {colloquial} slow-witted, flaky ◊ comparable ◊ peer, equal ◊ different ◊ doubt, hesitate ◊ change

F

饭店 fàndiàn ◊ restaurant ◊ hotel
飞机 fēijī ◊ airplane, aircraft
分钟 fēnzhōng ◊ minute (unit of time)

G

高兴 gāoxìng ◊ happy, glad ◊ be happy to, be glad to

个 gè ◊ {measure word} (usually pronounced in the qīngshēng 輕聲/轻声 "light tone") (used before a noun not having a dedicated measure word of its own, e.g., sān gè xīngqī 三個星期/三个星期 "three weeks", liǎng gè wèntí 兩個問題/两个问题 "two questions/problems") ◊ (contraction of yī gè 一個/一个, used between a verb and its object) a... ◊ (pronounced with full fourth tone) individual

工作 gōngzuò ◊ (do) work ◊ occupation, job, work

狗 gǒu ◊ dog, Canis lupus familiaris ◊ {abusive} damned (person, etc.); lackey

H

汉语 Hànyǔ ◊ Chinese, the Chinese (spoken) language

好 hǎo ◊ good, nice, fine ◊ good to (eat, etc.) ◊ be well, in good health ◊ (before a verb) easy to... ◊ (as a verb complement, indicates finishing or finishing satisfactorily) be done...ing, finish...ing ◊ in order to, so that, for the purpose of ◊ {regional} may, can, should, ought to ◊ (emphasizes the meaning of adjectives) very, quite, pretty much... ◊ (used before adjectives to inquire about quantity or degree) how...(long, far, etc.)?

号 hào ◊ name, title, style name, assumed name, alias, literary name, sobriquet ◊ firm, business house ◊ sequence, kind, sort, type ◊ person of a certain type (as in bìnghào 病號/病号 "person on the sick list") ◊ number ◊ (after numerals) number..., day of the month, street number, house number ◊ {measure word} (for large numbers of people, transactions, deals, etc.) ◊ put a mark on, number, give a number to ◊ sign, signal ◊ size (of shoes, clothing, etc.) ◊ count, measure (as in hàomài 號脈/号脉 "feel the pulse") ◊ indicates the name of a ship, spacecraft, etc. (as in Qǐyè hào 企業號/企业号 the "Enterprise") ◊ horn, trumpet, bugle ◊ bugle call

喝 hē ◊ drink ◊ drink alcoholic beverages

和 hé ◊ and; with ◊ together with ◊ kind, gentle, mild; (be) on good terms with, harmonious; harmony, peace ◊ {sports} (of the result of a competition) a draw, a tie ◊ Japan, Japanese ◊ He (surname)

很 hěn ◊ very, quite (often used as a rhetorical prefix to an adjective, with little or no intensification of the adjective's meaning)

后面 hòumian ◊ at the back ◊ afterwards, later

回 huí ◊ return, go or come back ◊ wind around, circle/turn around, look back ◊ answer, reply ◊ report (to a higher authority) ◊ go contrary to, cancel, dismiss, decline (an invitation, offer, etc.) ◊ {measure word}... times (for the number of occurrences, times, occasions, etc.); {measure word} (used for chapters, sections, sessions [of books, etc.], matters, occasions) ◊ the Hui (Muslim) nationality ◊ Hui (surname)

会 huì ◊ meeting ◊ meet with ◊ can, could ◊ understand, know (like a language) ◊ be able to ◊ will, be likely to, be possible, possibly ◊ moment, short while ◊ Hui (surname)

J

几 jǐ ◊ How many? ◊ a few, several, some

家 jiā ◊ family, household; home, residence ◊ (as suffix) expert/specialist in a certain field (like zuòjiā 作家 "writer") ◊ {philosophy} school (of thought) (like rújiā 儒家 "the Confucian school") ◊ party, side ◊ {humble} my... ◊ {regional} (of animals) tamed, broken, domesticated ◊ {measure word} (used for families, companies, hotels, stores, etc.) ◊ Jia (surname)

叫 jiào ◊ shout, yell, cry ◊ call out to, greet, address ◊ hire (like a taxi), order (a meal, dish, etc.), get ◊ name, call, designate, summon; be called/named ◊ ask, order, make (sb do sth), order, ask ◊ allow, permit, let ◊ by (particle used to indicate the passive voice) ◊ {regional} male (animal or fowl)

今天 jīntiān ◊ today ◊ the present, now

九 jiǔ ◊ nine, 9 ◊ {Chinese calendar} any of the nine-day periods starting the day after the winter solstice ◊ many, numerous

K

开 kāi ◇ open, open up, reclaim ◇ turn on (a light, the TV, a switch, etc.), be on ◇ operate, run (a machine, etc.) ◇ boil (water), boiled (water) ◇ lift (a restriction, ban, etc.) ◇ (of troops) move (in...) ◇ start, begin, set up (like a restaurant, shop, etc.) ◇ hold (a meeting, party, etc.) ◇ write, make out (like a prescription, receipt) ◇ pay (wages, a salary, etc.) ◇ (of a waterway) thaw, become navigable ◇ {regional} kick out, sack, fire ◇ (as a verb suffix)... far and wide; start (doing sth) ◇ rough percentage, approximate proportion ◇ {printing} folio (unit of paper size) ◇ Kai (surname)

看 kàn ◇ look, see, read ◇ think, view (the situation) ◇ visit, call on (friends, etc.)

看见 kànjian ◇ see, notice

块 kuài ◇ piece, lump ◇ {measure word}... piece(s)/lump(s) of... (used for money, things that come in a piece, and various thin and flat objects) ◇ "Yuan", "Dollar", etc. (unit of Chinese currency) ◇ {colloquial, business/administrative jargon} area, matter, aspect (e.g., wǎngshàng xiāoshòu zhè yī kuài 網上銷售這一塊/网上销售这一块, "the area of online sales")

L

来 lái ◇ come, come hither ◇ arrive (of seasons, etc.) ◇ arise, crop up (of problems, etc.) ◇ cause to come, let come, I'll have... (used in ordering in a restaurant) ◇ cause to arrive or take place ◇ for the past (amount of time) ◇ in order to (take some action) ◇ (following numbers) approximately ◇ (verb suffix) ◇ Lai (surname)

老师 lǎoshī ◇ teacher, professor ◇ master (form of address to a scholar)

了 le ◇ already (aspect particle indicating change) ◇ (aspect particle for new situation; verb suffix indicating an action has happened or is about to happen)

冷 lěng ◇ cold ◇ icy, cold, frosty ◇ Leng (surname)

里 lǐ ◇ in, inside (as a postposition)

六 liù ◇ six ◇ {music} Liu (a note on the Chinese musical scale gōngchěpǔ 工尺譜/工尺谱) ◇ Liu (surname)

M

妈妈 māma ◊ mother, mom
吗 ma ◊ "Is it...?" (sentence-final question particle)
买 mǎi ◊ buy, purchase
猫 māo ◊ cat (domestic cat, house cat, Felis silvestris catus) ◊ {dialect} hide, go into hiding
没 méi ◊ not exist, not have, not be there, be without ◊ there is not ◊ not as... as ◊ not... than ◊ scarcely ◊ less than ◊ not yet ◊ did not ‖ (used like méiyǒu 没有/没有)
关系 guānxi ◊ relation(ship) ◊ bearing, importance, impact ◊ involve, concern, have a bearing on ◊ (in a pattern like yóuyú... de guānxi 由於 … 的關係/由于 … 的关系, "owing to...", "on account of...") reason; (personal) connections, personal relations (usually backdoor)
没有 méiyǒu ◊ not exist, not have ◊ there is not ◊ not as... as ◊ less than ◊ did not, has not ‖ (same meaning as méi 没/没)
米饭 mǐfàn ◊ cooked rice
名字 míngzi ◊ given name, personal name ◊ name
明天 míngtiān ◊ tomorrow ◊ {figurative} the future, someday ◊ {classical} moon-lit sky

N

哪 nǎ ◊ (as interrogative particle, mostly followed by a number or measure word) which (one)? what? any ◊ (as a rhetorical question particle) how can...! how could...!
哪儿 nǎr ◊ where?; wherever ◊ {colloquial} "I don't think so!" (phrase used as a rhetorical question to indicate disbelief, a negative response, etc.)
那 nà ◊ that (one) ◊ then, in that case
呢 ne ◊ is it so? isn't it? how about...? and...? (question particle used at the end of a question) ◊ surely, certainly (sentence-final particle giving emphasis to a statement) ◊ -ing (at the end of a statement expresses that the action is continuing) ◊ well,... ◊ but (on the other hand)...(interjection used to pause a sentence, often to indicate a contrast)
能 néng ◊ can ◊ be possible ◊ capable ◊ energy (such as in yuánzǐnéng 原子能 "atomic energy")
你 nǐ ◊ you (second person, singular) ◊ one, anyone, a person
年 nián ◊ year ◊ yearly, annual ◊ age ◊ period of life (like childhood, middle age) ◊ age, period (of history) ◊ harvest ◊ New Year, lunisolar New Year season ◊ (of special items) for the (lunisolar) New Year (like cakes, painting) ◊ (of friendship, etc.) between those who passed the Imperial examinations in the same year ◊ Nian (surname)
女儿 nǚ'ér ◊ daughter, girl ◊ unmarried woman ◊ virgin

P

朋友 péngyou ◊ friend
漂亮 piàoliang ◊ good-looking, attractive, pretty, handsome ◊ (used to praise the way sb does sth) nice, outstanding, brilliant, splendid
苹果 píngguǒ ◊ apple

Q

七 qī ◊ seven, 7 ◊ {Buddhism} sacrifices held every seven days after death until the forty-ninth day ◊ rhyming prose ◊ Qi (surname)
前面 qiánmian ◊ in front, ahead ◊ preceding, previously
钱 qián ◊ money; cash ◊ coin ◊ {unit of weight} qian (approx. equivalent to 5 grams) ◊ Qian (surname)
请 qǐng ◊ request, ask ◊ please ◊ invite; treat (sb to dinner, etc.) ◊ engage, hire, retain (a teacher, nurse, lawyer, fengshui consultant, etc.); send for (a doctor, etc.) ◊ {archaic} buy (incense, candles, and various other accessories for religious worship) ◊ call on, pay one's respects
去 qù ◊ go (to), go away, leave, depart ◊ get rid of, remove ◊ (verb suffix indicating movement to a place)

R

热 rè ◊ hot ◊ ardent, fervent ◊ crave, be envious ◊ popular, in demand ◊ fad, craze, rage ◊ thermal ◊ {med} hot (one of the Eight Principal Syndromes, see Bā Gāng 八綱/八纲)
人 rén ◊ person(s), human being(s), people, man ◊ somebody else, the others ◊ Ren (surname)
认识 rènshi ◊ know, understand, recognize ◊ knowledge, understanding, cognition

S

三 sān ◊ three, 3 ◊ several, numerous, many (the character 叁 is also used in Simplified character mode, to avoid forgery)
商店 shāngdiàn ◊ shop, store
上 shàng ◊ on, on top of... ◊ last, the previous (like shàng [gè] xīngqīwǔ 上[個]星期五 "last Friday") ◊ first (in a series) ◊ go up, go up to ◊ mount, board (a vehicle) ◊ go to, leave for ◊ submit, send ◊ bolt, lock (a door, etc.) ◊ (used after a verb as a resultative ending to indicate the amount or extent reached)
上午 shàngwǔ ◊ morning
少 shǎo ◊ few, little, less, scant, not enough ◊ seldom ◊ missing, lacking ◊ owe (money, etc.) ◊ a (little) while, a minute
谁 shéi ◊ who? ◊ anyone
什么 shénme ◊ what?; what kind of...? something, anything ◊ (used to express anger, surprise, censure or negation) ◊ (used to express disapproval or disagreement) ◊ (after a verb) for what, why ◊ (used to indicate an incomplete list) things like...; and so on, and what not ‖ in traditional characters, also written 什麽, 什麼, or 甚麼
十 shí ◊ ten, tenth ◊ complete ◊ perfect
时候 shíhou ◊ time (when), moment
是 shì ◊ be, am, is, are (equating two things) ◊ right ◊ yes (response when called on) ◊ {classical} this ◊ {classical} correct, right ◊ (in the pattern 是…是…) is it...or is it...? ◊ "Yes!" ◊ "Right!"
书 shū ◊ book ◊ letter, document ◊ calligraphy style, script ◊ write ◊ {literature} the Book of Documents (short for Shàngshū 尚書/尚书, or Shūjīng 書經/书经)
水 shuǐ ◊ water ◊ (preceded by a name) ... River ◊ rivers, lakes, seas; a flood ◊ liquid ◊ additional income; extra cost ◊ (of clothing, etc.) times being washed ◊ Shui (surname)
水果 shuǐguǒ ◊ fruit(s)
睡觉 shuìjiào ◊ sleep; go to sleep

◇ go to bed, turn in, retire (for the night)

说 shuō ◇ speak, say, talk ◇ explain, give an explanation ◇ theory, doctrine, views ◇ scold, criticize ◇ act as go-between or matchmaker, introduce ◇ refer to, hint, indicate ◇ point to

四 sì ◇ four, 4 ◇ Si (surname)

岁 suì ◇ year ◇ years (old), years of age ◇ the year's harvest

T

他 tā ◇ he, she, it ◇ him, his (personal pronoun, prior to the May Fourth Movement [1919] used for all genders; now generally only used in reference to males, in cases when no gender differentiation is necessary, or when the gender is unknown; this is also the standard usage in Taiwan) ◇ other, another (as in tārì 他日 "on another day")

她 tā ◇ she (third person singular, feminine) ◇ her ◇ {formal} she (as a reference to one's country, party, flag, etc.)

太 tài ◇ too, excessively ◇ so, extremely (used in an exclamatory clause) ◇ greatest, highest ◇ Tai (surname)

天气 tiānqì ◇ the weather

听 tīng ◇ hear, listen ◇ obey, heed, comply with, take sb's advice/suggestion ◇ administer (affairs of state, justice), manage ◇ allow, permit (formerly pronounced "tìng") ◇ sb's ears/informer ◇ {measure word, phonetic}... tin(s) of...,... can(s) of... (from the English "tin"; used for items in tin containers or cans, like biscuits, cigarettes, beer, etc.)

同学 tóngxué ◇ fellow student, classmate, schoolmate; attend the same school, be classmates ◇ (form of address used when speaking to a student)

W

喂　wèi　◊ hello (or other interjection to attract sb's attention)
我　wǒ　◊ I, me; my ◊ {written} we; our ◊ {written} our country (usu. referring to China); our country's ◊ self ◊ Wo (surname)
我们wǒmen　◊ we, us, our
五　wǔ　◊ five, 5 ◊ Wu (surname)

X

喜欢xǐhuān　◊ like, be fond of ◊ be happy, be delighted, be filled with joy (also pronounced xǐhuan)
下　xià　◊ under, below, underneath ◊ the later, latter, last in a series ◊ the last part (of a work) ◊ next ◊ down, downward ◊ descend, go down ◊ (of rain, snow, etc.) fall ◊ send down (like documents); issue, deliver (like an order, an ultimatum, etc.) ◊ leave/exit (from) ◊ put in ◊ play (board games) ◊ take away, dismantle ◊ (of animals) give birth to, lay (eggs) ◊ defeat, capture ◊ yield, give up, give in ◊ get off/finish (one's shift) ◊ {measure word} (used for the number of occurrences) ◊ {measure word}... glassful(s) of... (used for fillings of containers like glasses, bowls, etc.)
下午xiàwǔ　◊ afternoon
下雨xiàyǔ　◊ rain (falling, as a verb)
先生xiānsheng　◊ (preceded by a surname:) Mr. ◊ Mister ◊ teacher ◊ (used together with personal pronouns, e.g., preceded by wǒ 我 "my...":) husband ◊ sir ◊ doctor ◊ (old meanings:) bookkeeper, accountant ◊ (used to refer to) people engaged in storytelling, fortunetelling, geomancy, etc.
现在xiànzài　◊ now ◊ nowadays, today, at the present time
想　xiǎng　◊ think (of); intend; be keen on sth ◊ want to, would like to ◊ long for, recall with fondness, miss, think of ◊ desire
小　xiǎo　◊ small, little ◊ my dear...(when used as [endearment] prefix, it can partially or totally lose its original meaning of "small")
小姐xiǎojie ◊ Miss (respectful term of address or title for an unmarried woman or girl) ◊ young lady (usu. unmarried) ◊ woman (used in terms for young women in certain professions, such as fúwù xiǎojiě 服務小姐/服务小姐 "waitress", kōngzhōng xiǎojiě 空中小姐 "[air] stewardess") ◊ {derogatory} call girl, prostitute ◊ {archaic} young lady (used by a servant in addressing his master's daughter)

些 xiē ◊ few, several, some (unspecified amount) ◊ somewhat, slightly ◊ (as a postposition, used to indicate plurality) ◊ {measure word} (used for an indefinite number of people or things, can only be preceded by the numeral yī 一 "one")
写 xiě ◊ write, compose ◊ draw, paint, sketch ◊ portray, depict
谢谢 xièxie ◊ thank you ◊ to thank
星期 xīngqī ◊ week ◊ Sunday ◊ wedding day ◊ the seventh day of the seventh lunisolar month
学生 xuésheng ◊ student, pupil ◊ disciple ◊ (your) student (self-designation when addressing one's teacher, master or a member of older generation) ◊ boy
学习 xuéxí ◊ study, learn ◊ learn (from sb), follow the example (of sb)
学校 xuéxiào ◊ school

Y

一 yī ◊ one, 1 ◊ alone ◊ whole ◊ once... ◊ Yi (surname)
一点儿 yīdiǎnr ◊ a bit, a little, some, a few ◊ a point ◊ {grammar} (a bit) more... (following an adjective, used to form the comparative, e.g., hǎo yī diǎnr 好一點兒/好一点儿 "[somewhat] better", dà yī diǎnr 大一點兒/大一点儿 "[a little] larger", etc.)
衣服 yīfu ◊ clothes, clothing
医生 yīshēng ◊ doctor, physician
医院 yīyuàn ◊ hospital, clinic
椅子 yǐzi ◊ chair
有 yǒu ◊ there is (are, were, etc.); be there, exist ◊ have, own, possess ◊ You (surname)
月 yuè ◊ month ◊ moon ◊ Yue (surname)

Z

再见 zàijiàn ◊ good-bye, see you again ◊ meet again

在 zài ◊ in, on, at ◊ exist, be present, be alive ◊ be in a certain category or class (as in zài suǒ bùmiǎn 在所不免 "is [one of those things that is] unavoidable") ◊ Zai (surname)

怎么 zěnme ◊ how, in what way, by what means ◊ why, how come, how is it that... ◊ what? (used to preface a sentence, expressing surprise, incredulity, etc.)

怎么样 zěnmeyàng ◊ What? How? How come? How about?; what, what kind of... (asking for a description, account, etc.) ◊ terribly good, terribly well (used in the negative)

这 zhè ◊ this, these (mostly preceding a measure word or number)

中国 Zhōngguó ◊ China

中午 zhōngwǔ ◊ (at) noon/midday

住 zhù ◊ live, dwell, reside ◊ residential ◊ lodge, stay at (as in an inn) ◊ stop, halt, cease ◊ {grammar} verb complement indicating that the action of the verb has been securely obtained, completed, etc. ◊ verb complement used after "de 得" (be able to...) and after "bu 不" (not be able to...)

桌子 zhuōzi ◊ table, desk ◊ {measure word}... tableful(s) of... (used for tables with dishes and wine, and for people seated at a table)

字 zì ◊ {linguistics} Chinese character, word, letter ◊ "style name" (name taken by a man upon reaching manhood, at around 20 years of age)

昨天 zuótiān ◊ yesterday

坐 zuò ◊ sit ◊ travel by, go by (car, airplane, etc.) ◊ (of a building, etc.) be situated/located ◊ sink, subside ◊ put a pot, kettle, pan, etc. on a fire/stove ◊ because, for the reason that... ◊ {archaic} be punished ◊ bear fruit ◊ become ill ◊ spontaneously, naturally

做 zuò ◊ work, do ◊ make, create, manufacture, produce ◊ be, become, act as, be used as ◊ write, compose ◊ play the part of, disguise oneself as ◊ hold (a celebration, like a birthday)

汉语水平考试

语法点

Grammar Points

HSK Grammar Language Points

HSK Level 1

The presentation of grammar points for HSK Level 1 is based upon the curricular outline in:

HSK 考试大纲 [HSK Test Syllabus], HSK Level 1, pp. 10-11. Published by the Confucius Institute Headquarters (Hanban). People's Education Press, Peking 2015. ISBN: 978-7-107-30418-7

There are 12 Language Grammar Point topics with eventual sub-divisions, all of which are listed on the following page.

Overview

Words and Phrases

1. Nouns
1.1 Time Nouns with 。。。的时候
1.2 Position Noun 前

2. Verbs
2.1 General Verb 在
2.2 Verbs of Potentiality and Will: 会, 能, 想

3. Pronouns and interrogative Pronouns
3.1 How much? How many?-Using 多, 多少, 几
3.2 哪 and 哪儿
3.3 Interrogative Pronouns Referring to Person, Things and Properties

4. Numerals
A. Expressing Amount of Money
B. Expressing Date
C. Expressing Hour and Minute
D. Expressing Age

5. Adverbs
5.1 不
5.2 都
5.3 没
5.4 太

6. Prepositions
6.1 和
6.2 在$_2$

7. Structural Particles
7.1 的
7.2 了
7.3 吗
7.4 呢

8. Interjection 喂

Sentence Patterns

9. Sentences with Nouns, Adjectives and Subjects as Predicates

10. Some Special Sentence Patterns
10.1 Sentences with 是。。。的
10.2 Existential Sentences with 是 and 有
10.3 Sentences with verbal constructions in series
10.4 Pivotal Sentences

11. Types of Sentences
11.1 Question Sentences requiring a YES or NO answer
11.2 Question Sentences requiring a "Content" Answer
11.3 Exclamation Sentences
11.4 Sentences Expressing Request

Complements

12. Complements of Result with 会, 好, 见

Suggested Further Reading

Words and Phrases

1. Nouns

1.1 Time Nouns with 。。。的时候

Structures with 的时候 express an action A that is taking place while another action B is performed or in progress. For example:

你<u>回来</u>的时候<u>买</u>些水果。
    Action A   Action B

In the sample sentence above, someone is asked to buy some fruit on the way home. Such structures are quite common in Mandarin Chinese, and Chinese grammar calls the entire complex of 你回来的时候 in the sentence sample above a "time noun". Such a time noun like 你回来的时候 is typically found at the beginning of a Chinese sentence. In English, such sentences would often translate in different ways paraphrasing "on your way home, buy some fruit".

1.2. Position Noun 前

Other grammarians might call 前 a postposition since it is attached to the end of another noun as the following sentence sample shows:

他一个星期<u>前</u>去中国。

一个星期 refers to a point of time ("one week") when X went to China. This point of time is further specified by 前 ("before" or "ago") that is attached to 一个星期. Chinese grammar calls this a position noun. There are other position nouns such as 后 or 旁边. Again as in 1.1 in the case of Time Nouns above, position nouns are attached to other nouns that make them then position nouns. For a complete list of time and position nouns, you should refer to systematic grammar books for foreign students studying Chinese as a foreign language like 外国人实用汉语语法 (修订本)[A Practical Grammar of Chinese for Foreigners, Revised Edition, published by Beijing Language and Culture University Press, Peking 2014, pp. 20ff].

2. Verbs

2.1 General Verb 在₁

You will typically find a verb like 在₁ in sentences like

他不在医院，他去学校了。
他在学校。
他在北京。

In sentence such as these, it is indicated that "X is in/at Y" with X usually referring to a person and Y referring to a location. The location usually follows 在₁. The major reason why 在 has a subscript 1 here is that it can occur in different grammatical roles as word in a Chinese sentence. In the sample sentences above, its role is that of a main verb. However, during the course of your Chinese language studies, you will realise that it can also assume the role of a preposition or a verbal complement. Compare for example the following sentences:

他在北京大学习汉语。
我住在北京。

In the first of the two sentences above, the sentence contains another main verb 学习 followed by an object 汉语. Here, 在 is a preposition indicating the place at which the studies are followed by X.

In the second sentence, 在 is attached to another verb 住 and assumes the grammatical role of a complement.

That means that 在 can assume several grammatical roles in a Chinese sentence:
- that of a verb
- that of a preposition
- that of a complement

You can now assign subscripts 1 - 3 according to the grammatical roles of 在. In this section, only its primary role as a main verb in a Chinese sentence is relevant. In this context, it may be of interest to note that many prepositions used in Modern Chinese were verbs in earlier stages of language development, and when losing their primary verbal meaning in the ancient language, they developed into prepositions in Modern Chinese.

2.2 Verbs of Potentiality and Will: 会, 能, 想

A. 会:
他会做饭。

The sample sentence above indicates that 会 is used as main verb referring to an acquired skill. Being able to cook is such a skill.

B. 能:
我在饭店，你几点能来？

The sample sentence above indicates that 能 is used as main verb referring to an instance of being able to do something that does not depend on acquiring a skill but on circumstances that a person may not always be able to influence. Being able to come at a certain time is such an instance.

能 can also mean "can/to be able to" with reference to a permissible or non-permissible action, e.g.

先生，这里不能打电话。 *Sir, you cannot/may not phone here.*

C. 想:
我想去睡觉。

In the sample sentence above, 想 is used in conjunction with another verb following it. This indicates that 想 acts as a modal verb here. It expresses a wish/desire to do something. The desire to go to sleep because one is tired is such an instance.

3. Pronouns and interrogative Pronouns

Overview: Personal Pronouns
我　你　他/她
我们 你们 他/她们

3.1 "How much/how many?"- Using 多, 多少 and 几

In Chinese, there are different ways of translating "how much?" or "how many?" It all depends on sentence structure and context in Chinese which of the following structural patterns would actually be used. Here are the patterns with some appropriate sentence samples:

A. 多 means *much* or *many*. It can occur in a sentence like
你女儿很漂亮。她多大？
where it simply means *many* and can refer to age.

B. 多少 literally means "many/much or few" and may be used when one doesn't have any clue about an amount at all, e.g.
你开出租车多少年了？

C. 几 can be roughly translated by "which"(A); in certain contexts, however, it may also translate as "some"(B).
(A) 你去北京几天？
(B) 这几本书多少钱？
It can often function as something like a place holder for days of a week as we shall see later.

3.2 哪 and 哪儿
哪 roughly translates as "which of X/who from among X" and occurs for example in sentence like this:
哪个是你的同学？

哪儿 simply translates as "where", e.g.:
你去哪儿？

3.3 Interrogative Pronouns referring to person, things and properties
谁 translates as "who?" in a sentence like
谁会说汉语？

什么 translates as "what" in a sentence like
今天下午你想作什么？

怎么 means "how" in a sentence like
下雨了，你怎么回去？

怎么样 also translates as "how" but refers to asking for certain states in a sentence like
你的汉语怎么样？

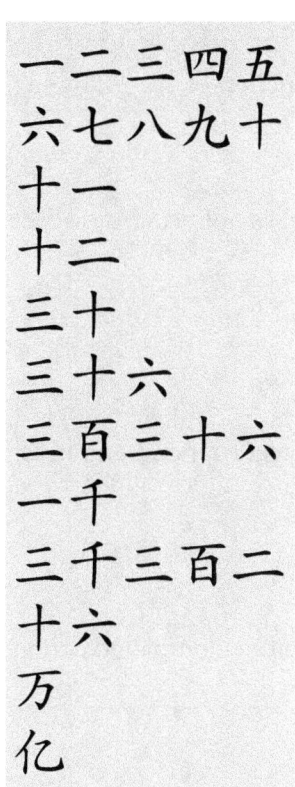

4. Numerals

There are different ways of expressing quantity in Chinese in addition to the use of numerals.

Small or really limited quantities can be referred to as 一点儿. It simply means "little/ a little/ a bit", e.g.

我会说一点儿汉语。

There are several other instances of expressing quantity in combination with Chinese numerals that are outlined below.

A. Expressing an amount of money with a numeral + 快钱, e.g.
六快钱
快钱 is a colloquial expression for the more formal 人民币.

B. Expressing date
In Chinese, the year comes first, followed by the month and finally by the day of a month. Optionally, the day of the week may be mentioned at the end of the complete date sequence, e.g.
一九九八年四月六号 星期一

C. Expressing Hour and Minute
Here again, the larger time unit precedes the smaller one. e.g.
一点十分

D. Expressing Age
Here, 岁 is used to express age; it follows the relevant numeral as in
四岁

Days of the week
星期日   星期四
星期一   星期五
星期二   星期六
星期三

Months:
一月   七月
二月   八月
三月   九月
四月   十月
五月   十一月
六月   十二月

5. Adverbs

At this HSK Level, knowing the meaning and grammatical function of the following adverbs is required:

5.1 不

不 is an adverb of negation used in sentences where either 有 does not occur or aspect indicated by 着, 过 or 了 is not marked, e.g.

我不认识哪个学生。

5.2 都

都 is an adverb translating as "all" most of the times in English. In English, "all" is a quantifier used before a noun while in Chinese 都 never can precede a noun and must always precede a verb. Look at the following sentence sample:

他们都是中国人。

5.3 没

没 is another adverb of negation and is used in sentences indicating completed action or states as in the following sentence sample:

昨天上午没下雨， 天气很好。

5.4 太

太 is an adverb expressing something or someone is in a state of abundance. e. g.
今天太冷了， 我不想去

6. Prepositions

6.1 和

In the following sentence sample below, 和 is a preposition that would translate as "with":

你和谁打电话？

和 can also assume other grammatical roles than that one. These will eventually be explained later.

6.2 在

在 is a clearly a preposition here and not a verb:
妈妈在那家医院工作。

There is a clear-cut rule for differentiating the grammatical roles of 在 as a verb or preposition in a sentence:
● When 在 functions as a verb in a Chinese sentence, there is normally no other action verb present. In this case, it translates as "am/are/is in/at...".
● When 在 functions as a preposition in a Chinese sentence, there is normally another verb present in a sentence.

7. Structural Particles

In Chinese, structural particles are also understood as "empty words" (of meaning) with certain entirely grammatical functions in a Chinese sentence. The following four structural particles can operate at different descriptive levels of a Chinese sentence.

7.1 的

的 is a structural particle mainly used to form various kinds of attributive sequences in noun phrases. It is also used to form possessive pronouns from personal pronouns. A simple structural formula is:

> Personal pronoun + 的 ------> possessive pronoun

A sample sentence is for example:

他的汉语很不好。

7.2 了

了 has basically these two functions:

a) It can assume the role of a sentence particle at the end of a sentence to indicate that a change in state has come about by the state, process or action expressed by the predicate. E. g.:

他去饭店了。

b) Following a verb as a predicate in a sentence, it can indicate completed action. For example:

他们买了很多东西。

7.3. 吗

Adding 吗 as a sentence particle at the end of a sentence makes the sentence an interrogative sentence that can be answered either with YES or NO.

你认识他们吗？

7.4 呢

呢 has several functions as a sentence particle.
a) In the sample sentence below, it may indicate some action in progress:
他在家作什么呢？

b) It may have a meaning of "what about..." at the end of a sentence as in the sample sentence below:
我爱吃苹果，你呢？ *(And what about you?)*

8. Interjection 喂

It may be used to call or address someone to attract his or her attention:
喂！你作什么呢？ *(Hello! What are you doing there?)*

It also used when replying to a telephone call:
喂！你找谁？ *(Hello! Who are you looking for [to talk to]?).*

Sentence Patterns

9. Sentences with Nouns, Adjective and Subjects as Predicates

Languages like English normally require a verbal predicate and a subject followed by the former to make it a meaningful and grammatically correct sentence. In Chinese, this is not always the case. There are the following exceptions:

A. A noun can function as the predicate of a sentence as in the sample sentence below:
In the sample sentence below, 星期六 functions as a sentence predicate:

明天星期六。

In English, a linking verb like IS would be required which is absent in a Chinese sentence in this case.

B. An adjective functions as the predicate of a sentence:
In the sample sentence below, 小 functions as a sentence predicate; a linking verb required in languages like English is not required:

他的衣服太小了。

太 is an adveb preceding 小 while 了 is a sentence final particle indicating change of state.

C. A sentence subject functions as a predicate of a sentence:
In the sample sentence given below, the subject of the sentence 天气很好 functions as a predicate in relation to 明天:

明天天气很好。

Note that in sentences with adjectives as predicates, the adverb 很 may be required to make it a grammatically correct sentence. This is always the case if the adjective is *relative* at meaning level and can be used in a comparative sense *(e.g., good - better - best)*. On the other hand, *absolute adjectives* at the level of meaning that cannot be used in comparative senses will not take the adverb 很 before them. Absolute adjectives, for example, are those referring to colour.

10. Some Special Sentence Patterns

10.1 Sentences with 是。。。的
是。。。的 is a grammatical frame construction to express emphasis of a place, a time or the manner in which an action was performed. It also implies completed action; and in English translation, the verb would then have to appear in the past tense form.

The following sample sentences express place, time and manner of completed action:

这些杯子<u>是昨天买的</u>。 *(Emphasis of time)*
我和马先生<u>是在飞机上认识的</u>。 *(Emphasis of place)*
他<u>是坐飞机来中国的</u>。 *(Emphasis of manner)*

The emphasised part usually is "embedded" within the 是。。。的 frame with 是 at the beginning of and 的 at the end of the emphasised sentence part.

10.2 Existential Sentences with 是 and 有
Sentences indicating the location of a person or object X at a place Y normally also imply existence of X. In the following sentences samples, 是 and 有 are used to express the existence of X at a place Y. The sentence subject in these sentence patterns usually is the location Y where X can be found. Grammatically, the sentence subject is a position or location noun; the second noun in the sentence following 是 and 有 is the object or person X said to be at a certain place Y.

Compare the following sample sentences:

这里面是什么东西？
桌子上 有一个苹果。

10.3 Sentences with verbal constructions in series
In this sentence pattern, a first action X is followed by a certain action Y in sequence or "series". Compare the following sentence sample:

她上午去商店买了很多东西。

In the sentence sample above, the first action performed is that "she went to a warehouse in the morning" with a subsequent action of "buying many things there". Chinese grammar calls such sentence patterns "sentences with verbal constructions in series" (连动句).
The same applies with respect to the second sentence sample below:#

他明天上午坐飞机去北京。

Note that a construction of <u>坐 + vehicle + verb of motion + place noun</u> as in the second sentence sample above indicates the manner of travel. If the travel is by plane, indicated by 飞机 following 坐, it is *flying*; if 坐 is followed by 火车, then the travel is by *train*.

10.4 Pivotal Sentences

In Chinese grammar, a pivotal sentence (兼语句) is one where the object of a simple sentence also is the subject of an "embedded" sentence. Such a Chinese sentence structure roughly corresponds to what is known as *accusativus cum infinitivo* (aci) in Latin and Ancient Greek Grammar. It also exists in other modern Western languages like English and German. A typical English sentence example would, for instance, be a sentence like the following: *I saw him come.* This sentence is a combination of the following sentence parts:

a. I saw X (X=b: he comes).
b. He comes.

Such sentence patterns also exist in Chinese. Compare the following sentence sample:
菜作好了， 去叫<u>你同学们来吃饭</u>。

11. Types of Sentences

11.1 Question Sentences requiring a YES or NO Answer
Question sentences that do not contain any of the interrogative pronouns usually are the ones requiring a YES or NO answer as in the case of the sample sentence below:

昨天的雨大吗？

The answers may perhaps look like that:
Either (a) 大。
or   (b) 不大。

Alternatively, this type of question sentence may be formed with the 大-不-大 pattern without the particle 吗 at the end of the sentence.

11.2 Question Sentences requiring a "Content" Answer
Unlike question sentences dealt with in 11.1, question sentences requiring a "content" answer contain an interrogative pronoun like 谁 (who?), 什么 (what), 什么时候 (when, literally: "which time"?), 怎么 (how?), 哪里 (where?), etc. Answering 谁 (who?) may contain the name of a person, answering 哪里 (where?) may contain the name of a place. etc. For the sample sentence below, the name of a person will be required:

这个人是谁？

In English, the difference between "Content" Question Sentences and those merely requiring a YES or NO answer is grammatically not really relevant while it is in Chinese: The former cannot contain a question sentence particle like 吗 while the latter must contain such a particle at the end of a sentence.

11.3 Exclamation Sentences
A special type of exclamation sentence is that using 太。。。了 with an adjective, for example, set between them: 衣服太漂亮了！谢谢你的. 太。。。了 expresses the speaker's attitude towards the high degree of a property that a certain thing expressed by the sentence subject is possessing. In the sample sentence, the speaker thanks the other person for a piece of cloth that looks "so beautiful/pretty".

11.4 Sentences Expressing Request
The formula 请 + Verb in Chinese expresses a simple, polite request that something be done on the part of the listener or reader. This is indicated by the sample sentence below:

请坐。

Complements

In Chinese grammar, complements are assumed to be immediate grammatical units of a sentence like subject, predicate, object, attributes and adverbial adjuncts. There are different kinds of complements, one of which is the complement of result, which in general expresses the result of an action.

12. Complements of Result with 会, 好, 见

The common structural pattern is: Verb + 会/好/见
For each instance, we provide the following sample sentences below:

A. Verb + 会
Verbs relating to the acquisition of a skill may have a following 会 as a complement of result to indicate that the learning process has been completed and the skill is now successfully mastered:

他学会了做中国菜。

B. Verb + 好
When 好 follows an action verb as a complement of result, it indicates that the action was completed successfully with a satisfactory result:

他做好饭了。

C. Verb + 见
When 见 follows verbs of perception like 听 as a complement of result, it indicates that the particular action of perception was or was not accomplished successfully:
我没听见。

Suggested Further Reading

Unless explicitly stated otherwise, all page references below are to: 《外国人实用汉语语法(修订本)》 (A Practical Chinese Grammar For Foreigners [Revised Edition]), Beijing Language and Culture University Press, 2014 [2008].

For Section 1 in this Book on Nouns:
cf. 外国人实用汉语语法(修订本)》, pp. 16 - 26

For Section 2 in this Book on Verbs:
cf. 外国人实用汉语语法(修订本)》, pp. 26 - 41

For Section 3 in this Book on Pronouns:
cf. 外国人实用汉语语法(修订本)》, pp. 95 - 105

For Section 4 in this Book on Numerals:
cf. 外国人实用汉语语法(修订本)》, pp. 58 - 73, pp. 73 - 95 (measure words).

For Section 5 in this Book on Adverbs:
cf. 外国人实用汉语语法(修订本)》, pp. 105 - 116

For Section 6 in this Book on Prepositions:
cf. 外国人实用汉语语法(修订本)》, pp. 116 - 123, pp. 213 - 222

For Section 7 in this Book on Structural Particles:
cf. 外国人实用汉语语法(修订本)》, pp. 131-145

For Section 8 in this Book on Interjections:
cf. 外国人实用汉语语法(修订本)》, pp. 146 - 150

For Section 9 in this Book on Sentence Patterns:
cf. 外国人实用汉语语法(修订本)》, pp. 334 - 353

For Section 10 in this Book on Special Sentence Patterns:
cf. 外国人实用汉语语法(修订本)》, pp. 557 - 558, pp. 496 - 504, pp. 477 - 484, pp. 485 - 495

For Section 11 in this Book on Sentence Types:
cf. 外国人实用汉语语法(修订本)》, pp. 368 - 395, pp. 399 - 401, pp. 396 - 399

For Section 12 in this Book on Complements and Complements of Result:
cf. 外国人实用汉语语法(修订本)》, pp. 271 - 329 and pp. 273 - 284 in particular

References

A. 孔子学院总部/国家汉办/**Confucius Institute Headquarters (Hanban)**：
《**HSK考试大纲**》/**HSK Test Syllabus:**

HSK 考试大纲 [HSK Test Syllabus], HSK Level 1, pp. 10-11. Published by the Confucius Institute Headquarters (Hanban). People's Education Press, Peking 2015.
ISBN: 978-7-107-30418-7

HSK 考试大纲, HSK Level 2, pp. 12-14. Published by the Confucius Institute Headquarters (Hanban). People's Education Press, Peking 2015.
ISBN: 978-7-107-30419-4

HSK 考试大纲, HSK Level 3, pp. 14-17. Published by the Confucius Institute Headquarters (Hanban). People's Education Press, Peking 2015.
ISBN: 978-7-107-30420-0

HSK 考试大纲, HSK Level 4, pp. 16-19. Published by the Confucius Institute Headquarters (Hanban). People's Education Press, Peking 2015.
ISBN: 978-7-107-30421-7

HSK 考试大纲, HSK Level 5, pp. 16-18. Published by the Confucius Institute Headquarters (Hanban). People's Education Press, Peking 2015.
ISBN: 978-7-107-30422-4

HSK 考试大纲, HSK Level 6, pp. 16-17. Published by the Confucius Institute Headquarters (Hanban). People's Education Press, Peking 2015.
ISBN: 978-7-107-30487-3

B. Complementary Sources Used:

《外国人实用汉语语法》, Beijing Language and Culture University Press, Peking 2014(2008).

《汉语语法百项讲练(初中级)》 [Chinese Grammar-Broken down into 100 items (Basic and Intermediate Level)], Beijing Language and Culture University Press, Peking 2011

《汉英双解新华字典》 [Xinhua Dictionary with English Translation], Commercial-Press, Peking 2000

吕叔湘 (Lü Shuxiang): 《现代汉语八百词》 [The Eighthundred Words of Modern Chi-nese], Commercial Press, Peking 1988

The Dictionary Definitions are taken from different high-quality databases included in the "Professional Chinese-English Dictionary" software, Version 2.0, downloadable from:
http://www.gelber-kaiser.de/ChinDict/Index.html (Freeware).

汉语水平考试

HSK Level 2

汉语水平考试

汉字

Chinese Characters

HSK Level 2
Character List

孩室帮思洗穿给药要贵送准哥息旁旅班病真离笑课唱啡常得您情教晚望球眼着票第

男纸诉走足身迎运近还进远间鸡事到卖咖备妹妻始姓宜房所泳玩知绍经表试非鱼便

向因场忙早次百红羊考肉自色行过问阴两但体别助吧告员完希床弟张快找报步每汽

丈也千已门为介从以元公夫手斤比牛长乐务可右号司外奶它左正瓜白让边件休共动

题颜篮

路跳错慢歌舞懂踢

等答跑道黑意新晴

累船蛋雪就晴最游

HSK Exam Level 2
Chinese Characters with Latin Hanyu Pinyin Transcription and English Meaning Definitions

丈 zhàng ◊ zhang (unit of length equal to 3.3 meters or ten Chinese feet) ◊ measure, survey (land) ◊ form of address to males either senior to oneself or related by marriage ◊ Zhang (surname)

也 yě ◊ also, too, as well ◊ (followed by a negative) (not) even ◊ nevertheless, still

千 qiān ◊ thousand, 1,000 ◊ thousands, great many ◊ kilo- ◊ Qian (surname)

已 yǐ ◊ already (short for 已經/已经 yǐjīng)

门 mén ◊ door, entrance, gate ◊ switch, valve ◊ hole/opening in human body ◊ family ◊ school (of thought), (religious) sect ◊ a teacher's or master's entrance hall ◊ means, method, key ◊ category ◊ {biology} phylum (of animals or plants) ◊ -gate (used by the media to create new words referring to a scandal, after the pattern of Shuǐmén [Shìjiàn] 水門 [事件]/水门 [事件] "Watergate") ◊ {measure word}... course(s) of..., ... subject(s) of..., ... skill(s) of... (used for school courses, skills, branches or subjects of knowledge, etc.) ◊ {measure word} (used for cannons) ◊ {measure word} (used for relatives, marriages, families related by marriage, etc.) ◊ Men (surname)

为 wéi ◊ be, mean ◊ serve as, act as ◊ become, turn ◊ do, act ◊ seem, appear ◊ by ◊ Wei (surname)

介 jiè ◊ lie between, be situated between ◊ act as intermediary ◊ an intermediary ◊ mind, take offense ◊ armour ◊ shell ◊ shelled aquatic animal ◊ (used with words denoting persons) a, an ◊ honest and just, upright ◊ {theatre} (in old drama scripts, word indicating motion or action)

从 cóng ◊ from ◊ through, since, by ◊ ever (before negation, e.g., cóng méiyǒu 從沒有/从没有) ◊ always (usually followed by 不, 沒/没, 未 etc. to mean "never") ◊ follow, accompany ◊ comply, conform, follow, obey ◊ act in a certain way (e.g., cóngkuān 從寬/从宽 "treat with leniency") ◊ attendant, footman, follower ◊ secondary ◊ cousin (relationship based on having the same paternal ancestor) ◊ Cong (surname)

以 yǐ ◊ in order to... ◊ take, use ◊ with, by means of, in, by (a certain means or fashion), at (a certain speed or rate) ◊ (used before the object of verbs with the sense of giving) ◊ because, because of...(a certain reason, excuse), on account of, given ◊ based on, considering, relative to, from the point of view of (a measure, standard) ◊ Yi (surname) ◊ [Yǐ] Israel (used as short form for Yǐsèliè 以色列, e.g., Yǐ Jūn 以軍/以军 "the Israeli Army")

元 yuán ◊ first, original ◊ chief, leading ◊ fundamental, primary ◊ yuan (unit of Chinese currency) ◊ Yuan Dynasty (1271-1368) ◊ Yuan (surname)

公 gōng ◊ public, collective, government-owned, state-owned; make public ◊ general, common ◊ official (affairs/business) ◊ fair, just, impartial, equitable ◊ (of measure units) international, metric ◊ (of animals) male (in contrast to mǔ 母 "female") ◊ duke (the highest of the five titles of nobility in feudal times) ◊ Gong (surname)

夫 fū ◊ adult man; husband ◊ man doing manual labour ◊ {archaic} conscripted labourer, corvée labourer

手 shǒu ◊ hand ◊ personally, with one's own hands ◊ person engaged in a certain task; person with a particular skill ◊ {measure word} (used for skill, dexterity, etc.)

斤 jīn ◊ {unit of weight} jin (equivalent to approx. one pound, or half a kilogram) ◊ character added to certain nouns to indicate weight ◊ pound ◊ {archaic} axe

比 bǐ ◊ compare ◊ than ◊ to (in a score, e.g., sān bǐ èr 三比二 "3 to 2") ◊ emulate, compete, match ◊ gesture, gesticulate ◊ ratio, proportion ◊ draw an analogy (with), liken (to), compare ◊ copy, model after ◊ {regional} aim at, direct towards ◊ {classical} close to, next to ◊ {classical} cling to, collude with ◊ {classical} recently

牛 niú ◊ ox, cow, bull ◊ cattle, bovine animals ◊ stubborn, obstinate ◊ {new Beijing slang} powerful; formidable, impressive; superior, brilliant; arrogant, cocky ◊ {physics} newton ◊ {Chinese astronomy} the Ox Constellation (one of the 28 Lunar Mansions, see Niuxiu) ◊ Niu (surname)

长 cháng ◊ long; length ◊ (one's) strong point(s), forte ◊ be good at sth, be strong in sth ◊ surplus, spare, extra (in this meaning, formerly pronounced zhàng)

乐 lè ◊ happy, joyous, cheerful ◊ joy, happiness ◊ be glad to, take delight/pleasure in, enjoy ◊ be amused, laugh ◊ Le (surname)

务 wù ◊ affair, business ◊ treat with priority ◊ be engaged in, pursue ◊ Wu (surname)

可 kě ◊ may, can, -able, be allowed to... ◊ possibly ◊ approve, agree ◊ need (to do), be worth (doing) ◊ {regional} do as much as possible, make the most of ◊ {written} recover, get well ◊ but, yet ◊ {grammar}(as an emphatic adverb used in an exclamatory sentence) really, indeed, finally; (expressing emphasis in a rhetorical question)...on earth...?; (expressing doubt in a question) really, actually? ◊ fit, suit, be agreeable to ◊ Ke (surname)

右 yòu ◊ right (-hand side) ◊ west ◊ Right (in contrast to Left [progressive, revolutionary]) ◊ advocate, uphold ◊ help, protect ◊ urge (sb to eat or drink) ◊ You (surname)

号 hào ◊ name, title, style name, assumed name, alias, literary name, sobriquet ◊ firm, business house ◊ sequence, kind, sort, type ◊ person of a certain type (as in bìnghào 病號/病号 "person on the sick list") ◊ number ◊ (after numerals) number..., day of the month, street number, house number ◊ {measure word} (for large numbers of people, transactions, deals, etc.) ◊ put a mark on, number, give a number to ◊ sign, signal ◊ size (of shoes, clothing, etc.) ◊ count, measure (as in hàomài 號脈/号脉 "feel the pulse") ◊ indicates the name of a ship, spacecraft, etc. (as in Qǐyè hào 企業號/企业号 the "Enterprise") ◊ horn, trumpet, bugle ◊ bugle call

司 sī ◊ be in charge of, oversee ◊ control, manage, operate, supervise ◊ bureau, department ◊ official in charge of a (government) department ◊ Si (surname)

外 wài ◊ outside, foreign ◊ except for, other than (often preceded by a phrase with chú 除......) ◊ unofficial (like history)

奶 nǎi ◊ breasts (of a woman) ◊ milk ◊ breast-feed, nurse, suckle

它 tā ◊ it (third person singular, neuter) ◊ other, another

左 zuǒ ◊ left (side) ◊ east ◊ left, progressive, revolutionary ◊ master, control ◊ unorthodox, queer ◊ wrong, false, incorrect ◊ opposite, contrary, different ◊ demote ◊ Zuo (surname)

正 zhèng ◊ straight, upright, perpendicular ◊ main, located in the centre, central ◊ (of time) punctually, exactly at, sharp, on time ◊ impartial, honest ◊ correct, right, proper ◊ (of colour, flavour) pure ◊ normal, regular ◊ chief, principal, prime ◊ {math} positive, plus ◊ rectify, correct ◊ right, just, exactly, precisely ◊ (as a particle indicating the ongoing action of a verb) in the process of... ◊ Zheng (surname)

瓜 guā ◊ melon, gourd, fam. Cucurbitaceae (the plant or fruit of various kinds of melons or gourds such as a watermelon, pumpkin, white gourd, cucumber, etc.)

白 bái ◊ (of colour) white ◊ (of daylight) bright, light ◊ (of facts, the truth, etc.) clear ◊ plain, blank, pure ◊ in vain, for nothing, futile, fruitless ◊ free (of charge), gratis ◊ (politically) white (symbolizing a counter-revolutionary or other undesirable political orientation) ◊ funeral ◊ give sb an unfriendly look ◊ {ethnology} the Bai national minority ◊ Bai (surname) ◊ say, state, explain ◊ {theatre} spoken parts (in a Chinese opera, etc.) ◊ {linguistics} (of Chinese text) written wrong or mispronounced ◊ dialect ◊ spoken (language), vernacular ◊ colloquial (vs literary)

让 ràng ◊ let, allow ◊ have or make (sb do sth), cause ◊ yield, give in, give up ◊ yield for, give (the right of) way to (e.g., another vehicle, pedestrians) ◊ let sb else have sth ◊ {sound transcription} Jean (French given name)

边 biān ◊ side ◊ border, edge, fringe ◊ trim (as decoration) ◊ border, boundary ◊ location, place ◊ Bian (surname)

件 jiàn ◊ {measure word}... piece(s) of..., item (used for clothing items, pieces of luggage, implements, utensils, matters, law cases, incidents, etc.) ◊ letter, document, piece of correspondence ◊ case (of bundled goods, such as soft drinks) ◊ {pottery/porcelain manufacturing} (standard measure for clay, used for measuring the size of vases)

休 xiū ◊ cease, stop ◊ rest, take a break ◊ resign, retire

共 gòng ◊ together, collectively ◊ common (with), general, universal; share, have or do in common; in common, in all, altogether, total ◊ (short for Gòngchǎndǎng 共產黨/共产党) Communist Party

动 dòng ◊ move, budge ◊ get moving, move into action, stir, act ◊ touch, displace, alter the position/shape of ◊ motion, movement (in contrast to jìng 靜/静 "still, calm") ◊ alter, change, modify ◊ use, put into use, make use of ◊ touch, move, sway, stir up, excite, arouse (like feelings) ◊ consume (food or drink) (mostly used with the negative) ◊ frequently, often, at every turn, easily

向 xiàng ◊ to, towards, from, against, towards ◊ side with, favour, take sb's part, be partial to ◊ (have) always, all along (literary equivalent of xiànglái 向來/向来 "[have] always, all along") ◊ {archaic} Xiang (ancient state during the Zhōu 周 Dynasty [1100-256 BCE], in present Jǔ Xiàn 莒縣/莒县 "Ju County", Shāndōng 山東/山东 Province) ◊ Xiang (surname)

因 yīn ◊ because (of), on account of, due to ◊ therefore ◊ cause, reason ◊ Yin (surname)

场 chǎng ◊ (gathering) place ◊ stage ◊ {theatre} scene (within an act) ◊ {measure word} (used for physical activities, athletic events, performances, dreams, exams, speeches, disasters, e.g., yī chǎng diànyǐng 一場電影/一场电影 "a (theater showing of a) movie") ◊ {physics} field (magnetic, etc.)

忙 máng ◊ (be) busy ◊ hurriedly, hurry to, hasten to ◊ Mang (surname)

早 zǎo ◊ early morning ◊ long ago ◊ early ◊ in advance, beforehand ◊ good morning

次 cì ◊ order, sequence, position (in a sequence),... times ◊ arrangement ◊ the following, second, next ◊ sub- (as in cìdàlù 次大陸/次大陆 "subcontinent") ◊ second-rate, inferior, shoddy, substandard, of low(er) quality ◊ {written} stopover, lay-over ◊ among, between, in the middle of ◊ {measure word}... time(s) (following a numeral, used for number of occurrences/times/occasions) ◊ Ci (surname) ◊ {chem} hypo-

百 bǎi ◊ hundred, 100; hundredfold ◊ numerous, all kinds of, all sorts of ◊ Bai (surname)

红 hóng ◊ red (colour) ◊ {informal} be popular, be "hot", be in great demand ◊ red cloth (hung to symbolize festive occasions, success, happiness, good luck, etc.) ◊ {figurative} (politically) "red" (i.e. Communist, socialist-minded, revolutionary) ◊ {economics} dividend, bonus ◊ (symbol of success) ◊ Hong (surname)

羊 yáng ◊ sheep ◊ Yang (surname)

考 kǎo ◊ test, examination ◊ take (and pass) an entrance examination ◊ check, examine, inspect ◊ inquire into, investigate, study ◊ {formal} one's deceased father

肉 ròu ◊ meat, flesh ◊ (of fruits) pulp, flesh ◊ {dialect} (of melon) pulpy, not crisp

自 zì ◊ self, oneself ◊ by itself, naturally, certainly, of course ◊ since, from ◊ start, beginning, origin ◊ because, due to ◊ Zi (surname)

色 sè ◊ colour ◊ look, expression, countenance ◊ kind, type, sort ◊ scene, sight, view ◊ (of merchandise, gold, etc.) quality, purity ◊ (mostly of women) good looks, attractive appearance ◊ sex, eroticism

行 xíng ◊ go, walk; travel ◊ trip, journey ◊ be all right, will do ◊ be capable/competent ◊ do, carry out, implement, perform (an action) ◊ behaviour, conduct, actions ◊ be current, circulate ◊ running script ◊ temporary, improvised, makeshift ◊ {written} soon, shortly ◊ {literature} ballad, song ◊ {written} (of medication) take effect ◊ Xing (surname)

过 guò ◊ go past, pass (by), go through, cross ◊ exceed, go beyond ◊ mistake ◊ blame or criticize sb for a mistake ◊ transfer (like money), adopt (like a child) ◊ read, go over, recall, call to mind ◊ {written} visit, stop by ◊ {regional} pass away, die ◊ {grammar} outperform, or fail (following dé 得 or bù 不 after a verb) ◊ {chem} per-, super- ◊ {regional} be contagious, infect ◊ Guo (surname)

问 wèn ◊ ask, inquire ◊ send one's regards, inquire after (sb's health etc.) ◊ Wen (surname)

阴 yīn ◊ {philosophy, Chinese med} Yin (the female or negative principle in nature, the opposite of yáng 陽/阳) ◊ the moon ◊ the north side of a hill ◊ the south side of a river ◊ {meteorology} overcast, cloudy ◊ shade (of a tree, etc.) ◊ the back side ◊ concave ◊ in intaglio ◊ covert, hidden, secret, inward, underhand ◊ gloomy ◊ sinister, perfidious ◊ of the netherworld, otherworldly ◊ {physics} negative ◊ {physiology} the female genitalia ◊ Yin (surname)

两 liǎng ◊ two, both (sides, parties, etc.) ◊ liang (Chinese ounce, equal to 50 grams) ◊ tael (unit of silver) ◊ liang (unit of 25 soldiers)

但 dàn ◊ but, on the other hand, nevertheless ◊ only, merely, just ◊ Dan (surname)

体 tǐ ◊ body ◊ substance (like solid, liquid) ◊ style (of writing or of Chinese characters)

别 bié ◊ other, another, different ◊ depart, leave, separate ◊ {regional} change, turn around ◊ distinguish, differentiate ◊ distinction, difference ◊ category, type ◊ stick into, obstruct (sb/sth) ◊ trip (sb), cause to stumble ◊ block (another bike or other vehicle with one's own) ◊ (contraction of the prohibitive bùyào 不要) "don't...!" ◊ Bie (surname)

助 zhù ◊ help, aid, assist ◊ benefit

吧 ba ◊ {grammar} "..., isn't it!" ◊ (sentence final particle, indicates consultation, suggestion, uncertainty, request, or command) ◊ (indicates agreement or approval) ◊ (indicates doubt or surmise) ◊ (indicates probability) ◊ (used within a sentence, indicates a pause after a supposition, a concession or a condition)

告 gào ◊ tell, inform, notify, report ◊ tell on (sb) ◊ {law} seek legal action against, accuse, sue, bring a case against ◊ request, solicit, ask for ◊ announce, declare ◊ announce/declare the completion (of a task, project, etc.)

员 yuán ◊ employee ◊ person performing a particular function, or engaged in a certain activity, profession, etc. ◊ {admin} member (of a committee, organization, etc.) ◊ {measure word} (used for military officers, and able/outstanding persons) ◊ border, perimeter

完 wán ◊ finish (the action of the preceding verb) ◊ Wan (surname)

希 xī ◊ hope ◊ rare, scarce ◊ pander to, cater to, silent ◊ Greece ◊ Greek ◊ will you please ◊ Xi (surname)

床 chuáng ◊ bed, couch, bench ◊ appliance or implement shaped like a bed ◊ chassis ◊ ground in the shape of a bed (like a seedbed, riverbed, etc.) ◊ {measure word} (used for bed covers, such as quilts, blankets, bedding, mattresses, etc.)

弟 dì ◊ younger brother; younger brother-in-law; male cousin ◊ {modest/humble} (in writing a letter) "I" ◊ Di (surname)

张 zhāng ◊ open, spread, stretch; extend a bow ◊ magnify, exaggerate ◊ look, glance ◊ {measure word}... sheet(s) of... (used for flat things like a sheet of paper, a table, etc.) ◊ {M} (for mouth, face) ◊ Zhang (surname)

快 kuài ◊ fast ◊ hurry up ◊ soon, shortly ◊ keen, sharp (-witted, etc.) ◊ content, happy ◊ Kuai (surname)

找 zhǎo ◊ search, seek, look for, try to find ◊ want to see (sb), call on, approach, ask for ◊ give change (money)

报 bào ◊ report, announce ◊ respond, reciprocate ◊ repay, requite, recompense ◊ newspaper ◊ periodical ◊ bulletin (like news bulletin), report ◊ telegram ◊ {Buddhism} retribution

步 bù ◊ step, pace ◊ (in a process) step, stage ◊ situation, condition ◊ {measure of length} bu (unit of length equal to five chǐ 尺 [Chinese feet], a Chinese foot being approx. 0.3 metres) ◊ {measure word}... step(s)...,... move(s)... (used for steps in walking and moves in chess) ◊ walk ◊ step on, tread ◊ pace off, measure by pacing ◊ Bu (surname)

每 měi ◊ each, every ◊ every time, whenever ◊ Mei (surname)

汽 qì ◊ steam, vapour, gas

男 nán ◊ man; male ◊ son ◊ baron (title in European nobility) ◊ baron (the fifth of the five ranks of nobility in feudal China of the past) ◊ Nan (surname)

纸 zhǐ ◊ paper

诉 sù ◊ tell, inform ◊ speak one's mind ◊ unburden oneself ◊ complain ◊ {law} accuse, sue, take to court ◊ appeal (like to a higher court)

走 zǒu ◊ walk, travel on foot ◊ run ◊ move, shift ◊ leave, depart (verb ending) ...away ◊ run away, flee, escape ◊ leak (out) ◊ lose the original shape, flavour, etc. ◊ through, from

足 zú ◊ foot, leg, base (of an object, like tripod) ◊ enough, sufficient ◊ full (amount, degree, etc.)

身 shēn ◊ (one's) body/life/person/character; oneself ◊ the frame, body (as of a car) ◊ {measure word}... suit(s) of... (used for suits of clothing) ◊ all one's life, one's lifetime

迎 yíng ◊ welcome, receive, meet ◊ meet head-on, confront

运 yùn ◊ motion, movement, freight ◊ convey, transport ◊ use, apply ◊ luck, fortune, fate ◊ Yun (surname)

近 jìn ◊ near (in time or space, in contrast to yuǎn 遠/远 "far, distant") ◊ close, intimate ◊ simple, easy to understand ◊ nearly, approximately

还 hái ◊ still, yet ◊ still more, even more ◊ also, as well, too, in addition, furthermore ◊ (when preceding an adjective indicating acceptable quality) passably, fairly, rather... ◊ (in rhetorical questions) even..., if... ◊ in spite of (sth unexpected, a difficulty, etc.) ◊ (to express emphasis) really, very ◊ (as a particle indicating grudging acceptance or unexpectedness) well then...

进 jìn ◊ advance, move forward/ahead (opposite of tuì 退) ◊ enter, come/go in ◊ take in, bring in, receive ◊ recruit, admit ◊ submit, present ◊ eat, drink, take ◊ (as verb ending) into, in ◊ {measure word} (of an old-style residential compound with an inner courtyard or multiple linked courtyards) a courtyard and its associated rooms ◊ {sports} goal (in soccer) ◊ {Chinese chess} advance (a number of points)

远 yuǎn ◊ far, distant, remote (in space/time) ◊ (of blood relationship, relatives) distant ◊ (of difference) far, by far ◊ not intimate, distant ◊ Yuan (surname)

间 jiān ◊ among, between ◊ interval; within a defined time/space ◊ room ◊ {measure word} (used for rooms)

鸡 jī ◊ chicken ◊ rooster ◊ {slang, Beijing} prostitute ◊ [Jī] Ji (surname)

事 shì ◊ affair, matter, thing ◊ incident, event ◊ accident, trouble, untoward event ◊ business ◊ work, function ◊ job, occupation ◊ concerned with, involved in, responsible for ◊ serve, attend to ◊ do, carry out, be engaged in

到 dào ◊ (from...) to, up until, up to...; as of ◊ arrive, reach ◊ (preceding a location) (go) to, leave for ◊ successfully..., succeed in...(verbal suffix indicating success of the verb's action, as in kàndào 看到 "get to see, notice") ◊ thorough, thoughtful, considerate ◊ Dao (surname)

卖 mài ◊ sell (opposite of mǎi 買/买 "buy, purchase"); sell out, betray ◊ outgoing, not holding back ◊ show off ◊ {measure word} (used for an order in a restaurant)

咖 kā ◊ {phonetic} ka- (used in the phonetic transcription of the word kāfēi 咖啡 "coffee")

备 bèi ◊ prepare, make ready ◊ make preparations, take precautions (against) ◊ have, be provided or equipped with, possess ◊ equipment, gear ◊ completely, fully, in every possible way ◊ perfect, complete

妹 mèi ◊ younger sister ◊ younger female cousin ◊ female relative of the same generation but younger than oneself

妻 qī ◊ wife

始 shǐ ◊ begin, start ◊ beginning, start (in contrast to zhōng 終/终 "end") ◊ first, earliest ◊ can only, only then ◊ Shi (surname)

姓 xìng ◊ surname, family or clan name ◊ the populace ◊ officials (in general)

宜 yí ◊ suitable, proper, fitting, appropriate ◊ should, ought to (mostly, but not always, used in the negative) ◊ of course, no wonder ◊ Yi (surname)

房 fáng ◊ house, building ◊ room, chamber ◊ any house-like structure (like a bee-hive) ◊ branch of a family; wife ◊ {measure word} (used for members of an extended family) ◊ shop, store ◊ {Chinese astronomy} Fang (one of the 28 Lunar Mansions) ◊ Fang (surname)

所 suǒ ◊ place, location ◊ (suffix indicating office, institute, etc., e.g. yánjiūsuǒ 研究所 "research institute") ◊ {measure word} (used for houses, schools, hospitals, etc.) ◊ {grammar} (particle used between subject and verb to indicate a doer-action-receiver relationship: (a) in a clause modifying a noun, e.g., tā suǒ xiě de shū 他所寫的書/他所写的书 "the books he wrote"); (b) used in the structure "sth 是 sb [verb] 的" ◊ (used after a phrase with bèi 被 or wéi 為/为 "by" and before the verb, e.g., wéi tā suǒ yòng 為他所用/为他所用 "be used by him") ◊ {written} used before a verb to form a noun phrase, e.g., jìn zìjǐ de suǒnéng 盡自己的所能/尽自己的所能 "do all one can, do one's utmost"

泳 yǒng ◊ swim

玩 wán ◊ play ◊ play with ◊ have fun, relax, enjoy oneself ◊ gaming

知 zhī ◊ know, understand, be aware (of), realize ◊ inform, notify, tell, let know ◊ knowledge, learning ◊ manage, administer ◊ close friend

绍 shào ◊ introduce ◊ continue, carry on ◊ pertaining to Shàoxīng 紹興/绍兴 city or county (Zhèjiāng 浙江

Province)
经 jīng ◊ through ◊ go through, pass through ◊ regular, frequent, constant ◊ the classics, the scriptures ◊ {physiology} menses ◊ hang oneself ◊ Jing (surname) ◊ {Buddhism} sutra ◊ the warp (in fabric, in contrast to wěi 緯/纬 "woof") ◊ longitude ◊ lengthwise alignment

表 biǎo ◊ surface, exterior; external, outside ◊ show, express, manifest ◊ form, table, list ◊ watch ◊ meter, gauge ◊ relationship between the children of a brother and a sister or of sisters ◊ gnomon (needle) of a sundial ◊ ornamental/ceremonial columns (erected before palaces or tombs) ◊ {historical} memorial (to an emperor) ◊ model, example ◊ {Chinese med} bring out/cure the cold with medicine

试 shì ◊ test, try, experiment ◊ test, trial, experiment ◊ try, attempt ◊ taste, try ◊ take up a post, assume an office ◊ use

非 fēi ◊ no, not ◊ (in compound words, as a prefix indicating negation) non-, un-, in- ◊ in no way ◊ wrong (in contrast to shì 是 "right") ◊ wrongdoing, evil ◊ negate ◊ not in accord with, not conforming to ◊ oppose, blame ◊ (often in the structure fēi...bùkě 非...不可) must, have to; be bound to ◊ insist on ◊ {written} degenerate, deteriorate ◊ (short for Fēizhōu 非洲) Africa, African

鱼 yú ◊ (a) fish ◊ Yu (surname) ◊ (a propitious symbol as homophone of yú 餘/余 "surplus, abundance")

便 biàn ◊ then, thus, in that case (consecutive particle, used similar to jiù 就, but more formal) ◊ (forming a hypothetic concession) even if ◊ convenient, handy, easy to... ◊ when the opportunity arises, when it is convenient ◊ ordinary, plain, informal ◊ urinate, defecate, relieve oneself; urine, excrement

孩 hái ◊ child, infant, kid

室 shì ◊ room, chamber ◊ house, building ◊ office, section, department (as part of a larger organization, like reference to room of a library) ◊ household, household possessions ◊ sheath, scabbard ◊ one of the 28 Lunar Mansions ◊ Shi (surname)

帮 bāng ◊ help, assist ◊ (of a bucket, ship, etc.) the side ◊ (of a shoe) the upper ◊ (of a head of cabbage, etc.) the outer leaves ◊ gang, clique ◊ business association of people from the same province ◊ {measure word}... group(s) of... (used for groups of people, etc.)

思 sī ◊ think, consider, ponder ◊ think of, remember fondly, long for ◊ hope, wish, desire ◊ (train of) thought, thinking

洗 xǐ ◊ wash, bathe, rinse, clean ◊ {religion} baptize ◊ remedy, redress, (set) right ◊ eliminate, get rid of, clear away ◊ kill and loot, sack (like a city) ◊ {photography} develop (a film) ◊ erase, delete ◊ shuffle (like deck of cards) ◊ small container for washing writing brushes

穿 chuān ◊ penetrate, pierce (through) ◊ pass through, go through, cross ◊ wear, put on (clothing), have... on, be dressed in ◊ to thread, string (like pearls, beads, etc.) ◊ {grammar} (verbal complement used after certain action verbs to indicate that the action was thorough and complete [e.g., kànchuān 看穿 "see through"])

给 gěi ◊ give, hand (to), present, grant ◊ (after a verb indicating transfer) to, toward; for, for the benefit of ◊ let, allow (also used as an emphatic particle, mainly in passive-voice sentences)

药 yào ◊ medicine, drugs, pharmaceuticals ◊ various chemicals (like gunpowder, solder, etc.) ◊ cure with drugs ◊ poison, kill (like rats, insects) ◊ {bot} Chinese herbaceous peony, Paeonia lactiflora ◊ Yao (surname)

要 yào ◊ want, need, desire ◊ demand, ask for, request ◊ must ◊ will, be going to ◊ need to, should ◊ it is necessary that..., one must... ◊ if ◊ if one hopes to..., in order to... ◊ (used in comparisons, for example 要比... yào bǐ or 比…要… bǐ...yào...), expresses a judgment/evaluation or highlights the difference ◊ important ◊ suppose that..., if, in case ◊ (yào..., yào...) either..., or.... ◊ Yāo (surname)

贵 guì ◊ expensive, costly, high-priced ◊ valuable, precious ◊ noble, of high status, of high rank, honorable ◊ {formal, honorific} your (surname, company etc.) ◊ (short for Guìzhōu 貴州/贵州) Guizhou Province ◊ Gui (surname)

送 sòng ◊ give as a present ◊ send, deliver ◊ accompany (like a guest to the door)

准 zhǔn ◊ standard, criterion, norm ◊ according to, in the light of ◊ accurate, precise, exact ◊ certainly, definitely ◊ quasi- ◊ {archery} the target ◊ zhun (musical instrument resembling the sè 瑟 "Chinese zither")

哥 gē ◊ elder brother ◊ "Brother..." (respectful way of addressing an elder male person; friendly way of addressing a male who is approximately of one's own age)

息 xī ◊ breath ◊ news, information ◊ stop, cease ◊ rest, take a break ◊ interest (on a loan) ◊ dividend (on shares) ◊ Xi (surname)

旁 páng ◊ side ◊ other, else ◊ {Chinese linguistics} radical (on the side/top of a Chinese character) ◊ wide-ranging, extensive

旅 lǚ ◊ travel, journey ◊ {military} brigade ◊ troops ◊ together ◊ set out, display ◊ order, sequence ◊ multitude (of people) ◊ lü (name of sacrifices to mountains, e.g., to Mount Tai) ◊ {divination} Lü (one of the sixty-four hexagrams in the Yìjīng 易經/易经 "Book of Changes") ◊ Lü (surname)

班 bān ◊ (of school) class, grade ◊ (of airline) flight ◊ shift, duty, work period ◊ squad (of soldiers) ◊ troupe, company (of performers) ◊ {measure word} a group of... (used for groups of people) ◊ {measure word} (used for scheduled trains, buses, etc.) ◊ (of a train, bus, plane, etc.) scheduled, regular ◊ recall, move, withdraw, re-deploy (like troops) ◊ distribute, give out ◊ Ban (surname)

病 bìng ◊ ill, sick ◊ disease

真 zhēn ◊ real, true, genuine ◊ really, truly ◊ sincere ◊ Zhen (surname)

离 lí ◊ distance (between, from) ◊ (following distance measure)... distant (from) ◊ leave, go away ◊ lacking, without ◊ Li (one of the Eight Trigrams in the Yìjīng 易經/易经 "Book of Changes") ◊ cut, sever ◊ meet with, encounter ◊ set out, display ◊ experience ◊ bright ◊ {musical instrument} li (large qín 琴 [guitar/zither]) ◊ Li (surname)

笑 xiào ◊ smile, laugh ◊ ridicule, deride

课 kè ◊ lesson, class ◊ {measure word} (for a lesson, unit of a textbook, etc.) ◊ administrative unit in certain organizations ◊ taxes ◊ levy, collect (taxes)

唱 chàng ◊ sing ◊ call or cry out ◊ song, the words to a song ◊ singing part of a Chinese opera ◊ Chang (surname)

啡 fēi ◊ {phonetic} -fei (used in the phonetic transcription of the words kāfēi 咖啡 "coffee" and mǎfēi 嗎啡/吗啡 "morphine")

常 cháng ◊ common, normal, ordinary ◊ constant ◊ frequently, often, usually, always ◊ {written} morality, code of conduct, rule of behaviour, principle ◊ Chang (surname)

得 de ◊ {grammar} (as structural particle between verb/adjective and a following complement) able to...; to the degree of...(used after certain verbs to indicate ability, possibility, or achievement to a certain degree, e.g., wǒ kàn de hěn qīngchu 我看得很清楚 "I could see it clearly")

您 nín ◊ you (polite form) (can be plural in certain contexts, as in 您二位 nín èr wèi "the two of you")

情 qíng ◊ feeling, sentiment, affection, emotion ◊ passion ◊ situation, circumstances, condition

教 jiāo ◊ teach, instruct (in most

compound words pronounced jiào)

晚 wǎn ◊ night, evening ◊ late (later than is proper/desirable), belated, delayed ◊ late, later in time ◊ junior; succeeding ◊ {formal} your humble junior (self-deprecatory term used in correspondence) ◊ {formal} in the latter part of one's life, in old age ◊ Wan (surname)

望 wàng ◊ look or gaze into the distance, look far ahead ◊ visit, call on ◊ hope, expect, look forward to ◊ prestige, renown ◊ towards, in the direction of ◊ (of age) approaching, near, almost ◊ resentment, enmity ◊ shop sign (on a flagpole) ◊ full moon ◊ the fifteenth (occasionally sixteenth or seventeenth) day of a lunisolar month ◊ Wang (surname)

球 qiú ◊ ball, sphere, globe ◊ {sports} ball, ball-like objects used in sports (like soccer ball, basket ball, ping-pong ball, hockey puck); ball games ◊ the world, the globe ◊ ball-shape things (like snowball, blood corpuscle) ◊ {slang, vulgar} "the balls" (as a term for the testicles)

眼 yǎn ◊ eye ◊ small hole; opening; eyelet ◊ sight, vision ◊ critical juncture, crux, key point ◊ {Chinese music} unaccented beat ◊ {measure word} (used for wells, springs, water taps, number of times one sees sth, cave dwellings, etc.)

着 zhe ◊ {grammar} (verb suffix, comparable to "-ing", indicating that an action is in progress); be -ing (used to indicate a state that is presently in existence and ongoing [e.g., mén kāizhe 門開著/门开着 "the door is open"]) ◊ (used after verbs or adjectives to make them more emphatic in meaning)... indeed ◊ (used as a suffix to form certain prepositions) (like shùnzhe 順著/顺着 "along", cháozhe 朝著/朝着 "facing, towards", etc.)

票 piào ◊ ticket ◊ ballot, vote ◊ bank note, (dollar, etc.) bill ◊ hostage held for ransom

第 dì ◊ number...(followed by a numeral, to form ordinal numbers)

累 lèi ◊ tired, exhausted, fatigued, weary ◊ fatigue, weariness, strain ◊ work hard, toil

船 chuán ◊ ship, boat, vessel ◊ Chuan (surname)

蛋 dàn ◊ egg (of a hen, bird, turtle, etc.) ◊ egg-shaped spherical object ◊ {ethnology} Dan, Tanka (boat dwellers in South China)

雪 xuě ◊ snow ◊ colour or luster of snow ◊ wipe away (shame, etc.), avenge ◊ Xue (surname)

就 jiù ◊ then, in that case ◊ on the subject of, with regard to, concerning, regarding, in connection with, as far as (sth is concerned) ◊ approach, move towards ◊ take up, enter upon, start doing (sth) ◊ comply with, yield to ◊ avail oneself of (sth at hand) ◊ at once, right away, in a moment ◊ (adverb indicating that a preceding number/quantity/time is relatively small/few/early) as early as, as long ago as, as soon as, as much/many as ◊ exactly, precisely ◊ only, merely, just, nothing (or no one) else than ◊ even if ◊ accomplish (sometimes used as a verbal resultative ending)

晴 qíng ◊ (of weather) clear, fine

最 zuì ◊ (the) most..., -est (prefix for the superlative, e.g., zuìdà 最大 "biggest")

游 yóu ◊ swim, float ◊ drift around ◊ part/reach (of a river) ◊ You (surname)

等 děng ◊ wait (for), await ◊ until, by the time when..., by the time that... ◊ {measure word} (used for grade, rank, class, degree) ◊ a (certain) kind, type, sort ◊ equal (to), similar ◊ {grammar} (plural suffix) ◊ and so on/forth/etc. ◊ {grammar} (used to indicate the end of an enumeration of items in a series)

答 dá ◊ reply, respond, answer; return (a visit, banquet, etc.), reciprocate; repay (a favour) ‖ (pronounced "dā" in certain compound words, e.g., in dāshàn 答訕/答讪 "say sth to smooth things over")

跑 pǎo ◊ run ◊ run away, flee, escape ◊ {regional} walk ◊ run around (on trips, doing jobs or errands, on business, etc.) ◊ (with an object like xīnwén 新聞/新闻 or xiāoxi 消息) cover (news) ◊ (of an object, etc.) get away, slip (away) (from the position in which it should rest) ◊ (as a verb ending) away, off ◊ (of electricity, oil, etc.) leak ◊ (of oil, gas) volatilize, evaporate

道 dào ◊ way, path, road ◊ line ◊ method ◊ morality, virtue, ethics ◊ {philosophy} doctrine, principle (of learning/religion/ethics), course, (the right) orientation, justice; Daoism (Taoism) ◊ superstitious sect ◊ {measure word} (used for narrow long shapes like rays, lightning, scars, door(way)s; for walls, instructions, [math] problems, [test] questions, courses or dishes of a dinner, steps in a procedure, coats of paint, times, repetitions, etc.) ◊ speak, say ◊ suppose, think ◊ Dao (surname) ◊ {admin} (during the Táng 唐 Dynasty) prefecture; (in Japan) prefecture (like Běihǎidào 北海道 "Hokkaidō"); (in North Korea) province ◊ {unit of measure} used for hūmǐ 忽米 "centimillimetre, one hundredth of a mm, cmm"

黑 hēi ◊ (of colour) black, dark ◊ secret (often illicit), shady, unlawful, clandestine ◊ evil, wicked, sinister, vicious ◊ unethical, reactionary, counter-revolutionary ◊ {colloquial} do sth unethical or unlawful ◊ (short for Hēilóngjiāng 黑龍江/黑龙江) Heilongjiang Province ◊ Hei (surname)

意 yì ◊ meaning, idea, thought, opinion ◊ desire, intention ◊ expect, anticipate ◊ suggestion, indication, hint, sign ◊ Italy; Italian (short for Yìdàlì 意大利)

新 xīn ◊ new ◊ modern, contemporary ◊ recently married ◊ newly, recently, lately ◊ Xin (surname)

睛 jīng ◊ the eyeball ◊ eyeball, look over

路 lù ◊ road, path, way; means, approach ◊ line, train (like of reasoning, thought) ◊ route, line ◊ Lu (administrative region during the Song, Jin and Yuan Dynasties) ◊ Lu (surname)

跳 tiào ◊ jump, leap ◊ beat, twitch ◊ skip (like a grade in school, a line when reading)

错 cuò ◊ wrong, mistaken, erroneous ◊ mistake, error, fault ◊ interlocking, inlaid, intricate ◊ stagger, alternate (like office hours, shifts) ◊ (preceded by a negation like bù 不) bad (bùcuò 不錯/不错 means "not bad", or "very good") ◊ {regional} except, with the exception of, but for... ◊ {written} inlay (with gold, silver, etc.) ◊ {tool} a grindstone for polishing jade ◊ polish jade

慢 màn ◊ slow (in contrast to kuài 快 "fast") ◊ postpone, defer ◊ haughty, arrogant, rude ◊ smear, daub ◊ {archaic} Man (name of a melody during the Tang and Song dynasties)

歌 gē ◊ song ◊ sing, chant
舞 wǔ ◊ a dance ◊ to dance ◊ Wu (surname)
懂 dǒng ◊ know, understand (like a language, what has been said, etc.) ◊ comprehend
踢 tī ◊ kick (like playing soccer) ◊ alarmed, frightened
题 tí ◊ forehead ◊ topic, subject ◊ title, heading ◊ write, inscribe
颜 yán ◊ face, facial expression/appearance ◊ face, prestige ◊ colour ◊ (inscribed) tablet ◊ forehead ◊ Yan (surname)
篮 lán ◊ basket (made of bamboo, etc.) ◊ basket (in basketball)

HSK Level 2
Chinese Character Stroke Order

字	部首	Definition and Stroke
丈 zhàng	一	①ten feet
也 yě	乙	①also ②too ③(in Classical Chinese) final particle implying affirmation
千 qiān	十	①thousand ②a swing ③a swing
已 yǐ	己	①already ②to stop ③then ④afterwards
门 mén	门	①gate ②door ③CL:扇[shàn] ④gateway ⑤doorway ⑥CL:个[gè] ⑦opening ⑧valve ⑨switch ⑩way to do something ⑪knack ⑫family ⑬house ⑭religious sect ⑮school (of thought) ⑯class ⑰category ⑱phylum or division (taxonomy) ⑲classifier for large guns ⑳classifier for lessons, subjects, branches of technology ㉑surname Men
为 wéi	丶	①as (in the capacity of) ②to take sth as ③to act as ④to serve as ⑤to behave as ⑥to become ⑦to be ⑧to do ⑨by (in the passive voice) ⑩because of ⑪for ⑫to ⑬variant of 為|为[wéi] ⑭as (i.e. in the capacity of) ⑮to take sth as ⑯to act as ⑰to serve as ⑱to behave as ⑲to become ⑳to be ㉑to do ㉒variant of 為|为[wèi], because of ㉓for ㉔to
介 jiè	人[亻]	①to introduce ②to lie between ③between
从 cóng	人[亻]	①from ②via ③passing through ④through (a gap) ⑤past ⑥ever (followed by negative, meaning never) ⑦(formerly pr. [zòng] and related to 縱|纵) to follow ⑧to comply with ⑨to obey ⑩to join ⑪to engage in ⑫adopting some mode of action or attitude ⑬follower ⑭retainer ⑮accessory ⑯accomplice ⑰related by common paternal grandfather or earlier ancestor ⑱surname Cong ⑲lax ⑳yielding ㉑unhurried ㉒second cousin
以 yǐ	人[亻]	①to use ②according to ③so as to ④by means of ⑤in order to ⑥by ⑦with ⑧because ⑨abbr. for Israel 以色列[Yǎsè liè]
元 yuán	儿[兀]	①Chinese monetary unit ②dollar ③primary ④first ⑤surname Yuan ⑥the Yuan or Mongol dynasty (1279-1368)

HSK Level 2
Chinese Character Stroke Order

字	部首	Definition and Stroke
公 gōng	八	①public ②collectively owned ③common ④international (e.g. high seas, metric system, calendar) ⑤make public ⑥fair ⑦just ⑧Duke, highest of five orders of nobility 五等爵位[wǔ děng jué wèi] ⑨honorable (gentlemen) ⑩father-in-law ⑪male (animal)
夫 fū	大	①husband ②man ③manual worker ④conscripted laborer (old) ⑤(classical) this, that ⑥he, she, they ⑦(exclamatory final particle) ⑧(initial particle, introduces an opinion)
手 shǒu	手[扌]	①hand ②(formal) to hold ③person engaged in certain types of work ④person skilled in certain types of work ⑤personal(ly) ⑥convenient ⑦CL:雙|双[shuāng],隻|只[zhī]
斤 jīn	斤	①catty ②weight equal to 0.5 kg
比 bǐ	比	①(particle used for comparison and "-er than") ②to compare ③to contrast ④to gesture (with hands) ⑤ratio ⑥Belgium ⑦Belgian ⑧abbr. for 比利時|比利时[Bǐlì shí] ⑨to associate with ⑩to be near
牛 niú	牛[牜]	①ox ②cow ③bull ④CL:條|条[tiáo],頭|头[tóu] ⑤(slang) awesome ⑥surname Niu
长 cháng	长	①length ②long ③forever ④always ⑤constantly ⑥chief ⑦head ⑧elder ⑨to grow ⑩to develop ⑪to increase ⑫to enhance
乐 lè	丿	①happy ②laugh ③cheerful ④music ⑤surname Le ⑥surname Yue
务 wù	夂	①affair ②business ③matter
可 kě	口	①can ②may ③able to ④to approve ⑤to permit ⑥to suit ⑦(particle used for emphasis) certainly ⑧very ⑨see 可汗[kè hán]

HSK Level 2
Chinese Character Stroke Order

字	部首	Definition and Stroke
右 yòu	口	①right (-hand) ②the Right (politics) ③west (old) 右 右 右 右 右
号 hào	口	①ordinal number ②day of a month ③mark ④sign ⑤business establishment ⑥size ⑦ship suffix ⑧horn (wind instrument) ⑨bugle call ⑩assumed name ⑪to take a pulse ⑫classifier used to indicate number of people ⑬roar ⑭cry ⑮CL:個|个[gè] 号 号 号 号 号
司 sī	口	①to take charge of ②to manage ③department (under a ministry) ④surname Si 司 司 司 司 司
外 wài	夕	①outside ②in addition ③foreign ④external 外 外 外 外 外
奶 nǎi	女	①breast ②lady ③milk 奶 奶 奶 奶 奶
它 tā	宀	①it 它 它 它 它 它
左 zuǒ	工	①left ②the Left (politics) ③east ④unorthodox ⑤queer ⑥wrong ⑦differing ⑧opposite ⑨variant of 佐[zuǐ] ⑩surname Zuo 左 左 左 左 左
正 zhèng	止	①just (right) ②main ③upright ④straight ⑤correct ⑥positive ⑦greater than zero ⑧principle ⑨first month of the lunar year 正 正 正 正 正
瓜 guā	瓜	①melon ②gourd ③squash 瓜 瓜 瓜 瓜 瓜
白 bái	白	①white ②snowy ③pure ④bright ⑤empty ⑥blank ⑦plain ⑧clear ⑨to make clear ⑩in vain ⑪gratuitous ⑫free of charge ⑬reactionary ⑭anti-communist ⑮funeral ⑯to stare coldly ⑰to write wrong character ⑱to state ⑲to explain ⑳vernacular ㉑spoken lines in opera ㉒surname Bai 白 白 白 白 白

HSK Level 2
Chinese Character Stroke Order

字	部首	Definition and Stroke
让 ràng	讠	①to yield ②to permit ③to let sb do sth ④to have sb do sth 让 让 让 让 让
边 biān	辵[辶]	①side ②edge ③margin ④border ⑤boundary ⑥CL:個|个[gè] ⑦simultaneously ⑧suffix of a noun of locality 边 边 边 边 边
件 jiàn	人[亻]	①item ②component ③classifier for events, things, clothes etc 件 件 件 件 件 件
休 xiū	人[亻]	①to rest ②to stop doing sth for a period of time ③to cease ④(imperative) don't ⑤surname Xiu 休 休 休 休 休 休
共 gòng	八	①common ②general ③to share ④together ⑤total ⑥altogether ⑦abbr. for 共產黨|共产党[gòng chǎn dǎng], Communist party 共 共 共 共 共 共
动 dòng	力	①to use ②to act ③to move ④to change ⑤abbr. for 動詞|动词[dòng cí], verb 动 动 动 动 动 动
向 xiàng	口	①towards ②to face ③to turn towards ④direction ⑤to support ⑥to side with ⑦shortly before ⑧formerly ⑨always ⑩all along ⑪surname Xiang ⑫surname Xiang ⑬variant of 嚮, direction ⑭orientation ⑮to face ⑯to turn toward ⑰to ⑱towards ⑲shortly before ⑳formerly ㉑to side with ㉒to be partial to ㉓all along (previously) ㉔surname Xiang ㉕variant of 嚮, direction ㉖orientation ㉗to face ㉘to turn toward ㉙to ㉚towards ㉛shortly before ㉜formerly ㉝to side with ㉞to be partial to ㉟all along (previously) 向 向 向 向 向 向
因 yīn	囗	①cause ②reason ③because 因 因 因 因 因 因
场 chǎng	土	①large place used for a specific purpose ②stage ③scene (of a play) ④classifier for sporting or recreational activities ⑤classifier for number of exams ⑥threshing floor ⑦classifier for events and happenings: spell, episode, bout 场 场 场 场 场 场
忙 máng	心[忄]	①busy ②hurriedly ③to hurry ④to rush 忙 忙 忙 忙 忙 忙

HSK Level 2
Chinese Character Stroke Order

字	部首	Definition and Stroke
早 zǎo	日	①early ②morning ③Good morning!
次 cì	欠	①next in sequence ②second ③the second (day, time etc) ④secondary ⑤vice- ⑥sub- ⑦infra- ⑧inferior quality ⑨substandard ⑩order ⑪sequence ⑫hypo- (chemistry) ⑬classifier for enumerated events: time
百 bǎi	白	①hundred ②numerous ③all kinds of ④surname Bai
红 hóng	纟	①red ②popular ③revolutionary ④bonus ⑤surname Hong
羊 yáng	羊[⺶]	①sheep ②CL:頭|头[tóu],隻|只[zhī] ③surname Yang
考 kǎo	老	①to check ②to verify ③to test ④to examine ⑤to take an exam ⑥to take an entrance exam for ⑦deceased father
肉 ròu	肉[月]	①meat ②flesh ③pulp (of a fruit)
自 zì	自	①from ②self ③oneself ④since
色 sè	色	①color ②CL:種|种[zhǐng] ③look ④appearance ⑤sex ⑥color ⑦dice
行 xíng	行	①to walk ②to go ③to travel ④a visit ⑤temporary ⑥makeshift ⑦current ⑧in circulation ⑨to do ⑩to perform ⑪capable ⑫competent ⑬effective ⑭all right ⑮OK! ⑯will do ⑰a row ⑱series ⑲age order (of brothers) ⑳profession ㉑professional ㉒relating to company ㉓behavior ㉔conduct

HSK Level 2
Chinese Character Stroke Order

字	部首	Definition and Stroke
过 guò	辵[辶]	①(experienced action marker) ②to cross ③to go over ④to pass (time) ⑤to celebrate (a holiday) ⑥to live ⑦to get along ⑧excessively ⑨too- 过 过 过 过 过 过
问 wèn	门	①to ask 问 问 问 问 问 问
阴 yīn	阜[阝左]	①overcast (weather) ②cloudy ③shady ④Yin (the negative principle of Yin and Yang) ⑤negative (electric.) ⑥feminine ⑦moon ⑧implicit ⑨hidden ⑩genitalia ⑪surname Yin 阴 阴 阴 阴 阴 阴
两 liǎng	一	①two ②both ③some ④a few ⑤tael, unit of weight equal to 50 grams (modern) or 1/16 of a catty 斤[jīn] (old) 两 两 两 两 两 两
但 dàn	人[亻]	①but ②yet ③however ④only ⑤merely ⑥still 但 但 但 但 但 但 但
体 tǐ	人[亻]	①body ②form ③style ④system 体 体 体 体 体 体 体
别 bié	刀[刂]	①to leave ②to depart ③to separate ④to distinguish ⑤to classify ⑥other ⑦another ⑧do not ⑨must not ⑩to pin ⑪surname Bie 别 别 别 别 别 别 别
助 zhù	力	①to help ②to assist 助 助 助 助 助 助 助
吧 bā	口	①bar (serving drinks, or providing internet access etc) ②to puff (on a pipe etc) ③onomat. bang ④(modal particle indicating suggestion or surmise) ⑤...right? ⑥...OK? ⑦...I presume. 吧 吧 吧 吧 吧 吧
告 gào	口	①to tell ②to inform ③to say 告 告 告 告 告 告

HSK Level 2
Chinese Character Stroke Order

字	部首	Definition and Stroke
员 yuán	口	①person ②employee ③member
完 wán	宀	①to finish ②to be over ③whole ④complete ⑤entire
希 xī	巾	①to hope ②to admire ③variant of 稀[xī]
床 chuáng	广	①bed ②couch ③classifier for beds ④CL:张|張[zhāng]
弟 dì	弓	①younger brother ②junior male ③I (modest word in letter) ④variant of 悌[tì]
张 zhāng	弓	①surname Zhang ②to open up ③to spread ④sheet of paper ⑤classifier for flat objects, sheet ⑥classifier for votes
快 kuài	心(忄)	①rapid ②quick ③speed ④rate ⑤soon ⑥almost ⑦to make haste ⑧clever ⑨sharp (of knives or wits) ⑩forthright ⑪plain-spoken ⑫gratified ⑬pleased ⑭pleasant
找 zhǎo	手(扌)	①to try to find ②to look for ③to call on sb ④to find ⑤to seek ⑥to return ⑦to give change
报 bào	手(扌)	①to announce ②to inform ③report ④newspaper ⑤recompense ⑥revenge ⑦CL:份[fèn],张|張[zhāng]
步 bù	止	①a step ②a pace ③walk ④march ⑤stages in a process ⑥surname Bu

HSK Level 2
Chinese Character Stroke Order

字	部首	Definition and Stroke
每 měi	母	①each ②every
汽 qì	水[氵]	①steam ②vapor
男 nán	田	①male ②Baron, lowest of five orders of nobility 五等爵位[wǔ děng jué wèi] ③CL:個|个[gè]
纸 zhǐ	纟	①paper ②CL:張|张[zhāng],沓[dá] ③classifier for documents, letter etc
诉 sù	讠	①to complain ②to sue ③to tell
走 zǒu	走	①to walk ②to go ③to run ④to move (of vehicle) ⑤to visit ⑥to leave ⑦to go away ⑧to die (euph.) ⑨from ⑩through ⑪away (in compound verbs, such as 撤走) ⑫to change (shape, form, meaning)
足 zú	足[⻊]	①foot ②to be sufficient ③ample ④excessive
身 shēn	身	①body ②life ③oneself ④personally ⑤one's morality and conduct ⑥the main part of a structure or body ⑦pregnant ⑧classifier for sets of clothes: suit, twinset ⑨Kangxi radical 158
迎 yíng	辵[辶]	①to welcome ②to meet ③to face ④to forge ahead (esp. in the face of difficulties)
运 yùn	辵[辶]	①to move ②to transport ③to use ④to apply ⑤fortune ⑥luck ⑦fate

HSK Level 2
Chinese Character Stroke Order

字	部首	Definition and Stroke
近 jìn	辵[辶]	①near ②close to ③approximately
还 huán	辵[辶]	①to pay back ②to return ③still ④still in progress ⑤still more ⑥yet ⑦even more ⑧in addition ⑨fairly ⑩passably (good) ⑪as early as ⑫even ⑬also ⑭else
进 jìn	辵[辶]	①to advance ②to enter ③to come (or go) into ④to receive or admit ⑤to eat or drink ⑥to submit or present ⑦(used after a verb) into, in ⑧to score a goal
远 yuǎn	辵[辶]	①far ②distant ③remote ④to distance oneself from (classical)
间 jiān	门	①between ②among ③within a definite time or space ④room ⑤section of a room or lateral space between two pairs of pillars ⑥classifier for rooms ⑦gap ⑧to separate ⑨to thin out (seedlings) ⑩to sow discontent
鸡 jī	鸟	①fowl ②chicken ③CL:隻|只[zhī] ④variant of 雞|鸡[jī]
事 shì	亅	①matter ②thing ③item ④work ⑤affair ⑥CL:件[jiàn],樁|桩[zhuāng]
到 dào	刀[刂]	①to (a place) ②until (a time) ③up to ④to go ⑤to arrive
卖 mài	十	①to sell ②to betray ③to spare no effort ④to show off or flaunt
咖 kā	口	①coffee ②class ③grade

HSK Level 2
Chinese Character Stroke Order

字	部首	Definition and Stroke
备 bèi	夂	①to prepare ②get ready ③to provide or equip
妹 mèi	女	①younger sister
妻 qī	女	①wife ②to marry off (a daughter)
始 shǐ	女	①to begin ②to start ③then ④only then
姓 xìng	女	①family name ②surname ③CL:個|个[gè] ④to be surnamed
宜 yí	宀	①surname Yi ②proper ③should ④suitable ⑤appropriate
房 fáng	户	①house ②room ③CL:間|间[jiān] ④surname Fang
所 suǒ	户	①actually ②place ③classifier for houses, small buildings, institutions etc ④that which ⑤particle introducing a relative clause or passive ⑥CL:個|个[gè]
泳 yǒng	水[氵]	①swimming ②to swim
玩 wán	玉[王]	①toy ②sth used for amusement ③curio or antique (Taiwan pr. [wàn]) ④to play ⑤to have fun ⑥to trifle with ⑦to keep sth for entertainment

HSK Level 2
Chinese Character Stroke Order

字	部首	Definition and Stroke
知 zhī	矢	①to know ②to be aware
绍 shào	纟	①to continue ②to carry on ③surname Shao
经 jīng	纟	①classics ②sacred book ③scripture ④to pass through ⑤to undergo ⑥warp ⑦longitude ⑧abbr. for economics 經濟|经济[jīng jì] ⑨surname Jing
表 biǎo	衣[衤]	①exterior surface ②family relationship via females ③to show (one's opinion) ④a model ⑤a table (listing information) ⑥a form ⑦a meter (measuring sth) ⑧wrist or pocket watch ⑨wrist or pocket watch
试 shì	讠	①to test ②to try ③experiment ④examination ⑤test
非 fēi	非	①to not be ②not ③wrong ④incorrect ⑤non- ⑥un- ⑦in- ⑧to reproach or blame ⑨(colloquial) to insist on ⑩simply must ⑪abbr. for 非洲[Fēi zhōu], Africa
鱼 yú	鱼	①fish ②CL:條|条[tiáo],尾[wěi] ③surname Yu
便 biàn	人[亻]	①ordinary ②plain ③convenient ④as convenient ⑤when the chance arises ⑥handy ⑦easy ⑧informal ⑨simple ⑩so ⑪thus ⑫to relieve oneself ⑬to urinate ⑭to defecate ⑮equivalent to 就[jiù]: then ⑯in that case ⑰even if ⑱soon afterwards ⑲advantageous ⑳cheap
孩 hái	子	①child
室 shì	宀	①room ②work unit ③grave ④scabbard ⑤family or clan ⑥one of the 28 constellations of Chinese astronomy ⑦surname Shi

HSK Level 2
Chinese Character Stroke Order

字	部首	Definition and Stroke
帮 bāng	巾	①to help ②to assist ③to support ④for sb (i.e. as a help) ⑤hired (as worker) ⑥side (of pail, boat etc) ⑦outer layer ⑧group ⑨gang ⑩clique ⑪party ⑫secret society
思 sī	心[忄]	①to think ②to consider
洗 xǐ	水[氵]	①to wash ②to bathe ③to develop (photo)
穿 chuān	穴	①to bore through ②to pierce ③to perforate ④to penetrate ⑤to pass through ⑥to dress ⑦to wear ⑧to put on ⑨to thread
给 gěi	纟	①to ②for ③for the benefit of ④to give ⑤to allow ⑥to do sth (for sb) ⑦(passive particle) ⑧to supply ⑨to provide
药 yào	艸[艹]	①medicine ②drug ③cure ④CL:種|种[zhǐng],服[fù],味[wèi] ⑤leaf of the iris ⑥variant of 藥|药[yào]
要 yào	西	①important ②vital ③to want ④will ⑤going to (as future auxiliary) ⑥may ⑦must ⑧(used in a comparison) must be ⑨probably ⑩to demand ⑪to request ⑫to coerce
贵 guì	贝	①expensive ②noble ③your (name) ④precious
送 sòng	辵[辶]	①to deliver ②to carry ③to give (as a present) ④to present (with) ⑤to see off ⑥to send
准 zhǔn	冫	①to allow ②to grant ③in accordance with ④in the light of ⑤horizontal (old) ⑥accurate ⑦standard ⑧definitely ⑨certainly ⑩about to become (bride, son-in-law etc) ⑪quasi- ⑫para- ⑬horizontal (old) ⑭accurate ⑮standard ⑯definitely ⑰certainly ⑱about to become (bride, son-in-law etc) ⑲quasi- ⑳para-

HSK Level 2
Chinese Character Stroke Order

字	部首	Definition and Stroke
哥 gē	口	①elder brother
息 xī	心[忄]	①breath ②news ③interest (on an investment or loan) ④to cease ⑤to stop ⑥to rest ⑦Taiwan pr. [xí]
旁 páng	方	①beside ②one side ③other ④side ⑤self ⑥the right-hand side of split Chinese character, often the phonetic
旅 lǚ	方	①trip ②travel ③to travel
班 bān	玉[王]	①team ②class ③squad ④work shift ⑤ranking ⑥CL:個|个[gè] ⑦classifier for groups ⑧surname Ban
病 bìng	疒	①illness ②CL:場|场[cháng] ③disease ④to fall ill ⑤defect
真 zhēn	目[罒]	①really ②truly ③indeed ④real ⑤true ⑥genuine
离 lí	凵	①mythical beast (archaic) ②to leave ③to part from ④to be away from ⑤(in giving distances) from ⑥without (sth) ⑦independent of ⑧one of the Eight Trigrams 八卦[bā guà], symbolizing fire ⑨离 ⑩surname Li ⑪to leave ⑫to part from ⑬to be away from ⑭(in giving distances) from ⑮without (sth) ⑯independent of ⑰one of the Eight Trigrams 八卦[bā guà], symbolizing fire ⑱离 ⑲surname Li
笑 xiào	竹[⺮]	①laugh ②smile ③CL:個|个[gè]
课 kè	讠	①subject ②course ③CL: 門|门[mén] ④class ⑤lesson ⑥CL:堂[táng],節|节[jié] ⑦to levy ⑧tax ⑨form of divination

HSK Level 2
Chinese Character Stroke Order

字	部首	Definition and Stroke
唱 chàng	口	①to sing ②to call loudly ③to chant
啡 fēi	口	①(phonetic component)
常 cháng	巾	①always ②ever ③often ④frequently ⑤common ⑥general ⑦constant ⑧surname Chang
得 dé	彳	①to obtain ②to get ③to gain ④to catch (a disease) ⑤proper ⑥suitable ⑦proud ⑧contented ⑨to allow ⑩to permit ⑪ready ⑫finished ⑬structural particle: used after a verb (or adjective as main verb), linking it to following phrase indicating effect, degree, possibility etc ⑭to have to ⑮must ⑯ought to ⑰to need to
您 nín	心[忄]	①you (courteous, as opposed to informal 你[nǐ])
情 qíng	心[忄]	①feeling ②emotion ③passion ④situation
教 jiào	攴[攵]	①religion ②teaching ③to make ④to cause ⑤to tell ⑥surname Jiao ⑦to teach
晚 wǎn	日	①evening ②night ③late
望 wàng	月	①full moon ②to hope ③to expect ④to visit ⑤to gaze (into the distance) ⑥to look towards ⑦towards
球 qiú	玉[王]	①ball ②sphere ③globe ④CL:個|个[gè] ⑤ball game ⑥match ⑦CL:場|场[chǎng]

HSK Level 2
Chinese Character Stroke Order

字	部首	Definition and Stroke
眼 yǎn	目[罒]	①eye ②small hole ③crux (of a matter) ④CL:隻|只[zhī],雙|双[shuāng] ⑤classifier for big hollow things (wells, stoves, pots etc)
着 zhe	目[罒]	①aspect particle indicating action in progress ②to wear (clothes) ③to contact ④to use ⑤to apply ⑥to touch ⑦to come in contact with ⑧to feel ⑨to be affected by ⑩to catch fire ⑪to fall asleep ⑫to burn ⑬to make known ⑭to show ⑮to prove ⑯to write ⑰book ⑱outstanding ⑲(chess) move ⑳trick ㉑all right! ㉒(dialect) to add
票 piào	示[礻]	①ticket ②ballot ③bank note ④CL:張|张[zhāng] ⑤person held for ransom ⑥amateur performance of Chinese opera ⑦classifier for shipments and business transactions (topolect)
第 dì	竹[⺮]	①(prefix indicating ordinal number, e.g. first, number two etc)
累 lěi	糸	①to accumulate ②to involve or implicate ③continuous ④repeated ⑤tired ⑥weary ⑦to strain ⑧to wear out ⑨to work hard ⑩rope ⑪to bind together ⑫to twist around ⑬rope ⑭to bind together ⑮to twist around
船 chuán	舟	①boat ②vessel ③ship ④CL:條|条[tiáo],艘[sōu],隻|只[zhī]
蛋 dàn	虫	①egg ②oval shaped ③CL:個|个[gè],打[dá]
雪 xuě	雨	①snow ②snowfall ③CL:場|场[cháng] ④to have the appearance of snow ⑤to wipe away, off or out ⑥to clean ⑦surname Xue
就 jiù	尢	①at once ②right away ③only ④just (emphasis) ⑤as early as ⑥already ⑦as soon as ⑧then ⑨in that case ⑩as many as ⑪even if ⑫to approach ⑬to move towards ⑭to undertake ⑮to engage in ⑯to suffer ⑰subjected to ⑱to accomplish ⑲to take advantage of ⑳to go with (of foods) ㉑with regard to ㉒concerning
晴 qíng	日	①clear ②fine (weather)

HSK Level 2
Chinese Character Stroke Order

字	部首	Definition and Stroke
最 zuì	日	① most ② the most ③ -est (superlative suffix)
游 yóu	水 [氵]	① to swim ② to walk ③ to tour ④ to roam ⑤ to travel ⑥ surname You ⑦ to walk ⑧ to tour ⑨ to roam ⑩ to travel ⑪ to walk ⑫ to tour ⑬ to roam ⑭ to travel
等 děng	竹 [⺮]	① class ② rank ③ grade ④ equal to ⑤ same as ⑥ to wait for ⑦ to await ⑧ et cetera ⑨ and so on ⑩ et al. (and other authors) ⑪ after ⑫ as soon as ⑬ once
答 dá	竹 [⺮]	① reply ② answer ③ return ④ respond ⑤ echo ⑥ to answer ⑦ to agree
跑 pǎo	足 [⻊]	① to run ② to run away ③ to escape ④ to run around (on errands etc) ⑤ (of a gas or liquid) to leak or evaporate ⑥ (verb complement) away ⑦ off ⑧ (of an animal) to paw (the ground)
道 dào	辵 [辶]	① direction ② way ③ road ④ path ⑤ principle ⑥ truth ⑦ morality ⑧ reason ⑨ skill ⑩ method ⑪ Dao (of Daoism) ⑫ to say ⑬ to speak ⑭ to talk ⑮ classifier for long thin stretches, rivers, roads etc ⑯ province (of Korea 도, and formerly Japan dō) ⑰ CL:條|条[tiáo],股[gǔ]
黑 hēi	黑	① black ② dark ③ (loanword) to hack ④ abbr. for Heilongjiang province 黑龍江|黑龙江[Hēi lóng jiāng]
意 yì	心 [忄]	① idea ② meaning ③ thought ④ to think ⑤ wish ⑥ desire ⑦ intention ⑧ to expect ⑨ to anticipate ⑩ Italy ⑪ Italian ⑫ abbr. for 意大利[Yì dà lì]
新 xīn	斤	① new ② newly ③ meso- (chemistry) ④ abbr. for Xinjiang 新疆[Xīn jiāng] or Singapore 新加坡[Xīn jiā pō]
睛 jīng	目 [罒]	① eye ② eyeball

HSK Level 2
Chinese Character Stroke Order

字	部首	Definition and Stroke
路 lù	足[⻊]	①road ②CL:條|条[tiáo] ③journey ④route ⑤line (bus etc) ⑥sort ⑦kind ⑧surname Lu
跳 tiào	足[⻊]	①to jump ②to hop ③to skip over ④to bounce ⑤to palpitate
错 cuò	钅	①mistake ②wrong ③bad ④interlocking ⑤complex ⑥to grind ⑦to polish ⑧to alternate ⑨to stagger ⑩to miss ⑪to let slip ⑫to evade ⑬to inlay with gold or silver ⑭surname Cuo
慢 màn	心[忄]	①slow
歌 gē	欠	①song ②CL:支[zhī],首[shǐu] ③to sing
舞 wǔ	舛	①to dance ②to wield ③to brandish
懂 dǒng	心[忄]	①to understand ②to know
踢 tī	足[⻊]	①to kick ②to play (e.g. soccer)
题 tí	页	①topic ②problem for discussion ③exam question ④subject ⑤to inscribe ⑥to mention ⑦CL:個|个[gè],道[dào]
颜 yán	页	①color ②face ③countenance ④surname Yan ⑤Japanese variant of 顏|颜[yán]

HSK Level 2
Chinese Character Stroke Order

字	部首	Definition and Stroke
篮 lán	竹[⺮]	①basket ②goal 篮 篮 篮 篮 篮 篮 篮 篮 篮 篮 篮 篮 篮 篮 篮

汉语水平考试

词汇

Words To Know

WORDS TO KNOW

B

吧 ba ◊ {grammar} "..., isn't it!" ◊ (sentence final particle, indicates consultation, suggestion, uncertainty, request, or command) ◊ (indicates agreement or approval) ◊ (indicates doubt or surmise) ◊ (indicates probability) ◊ (used within a sentence, indicates a pause after a supposition, a concession or a condition)

白 bái ◊ (of colour) white ◊ (of daylight) bright, light ◊ (of facts, the truth, etc.) clear ◊ plain, blank, pure ◊ in vain, for nothing, futile, fruitless ◊ free (of charge), gratis ◊ (politically) white (symbolizing a counter-revolutionary or other undesirable political orientation) ◊ funeral ◊ give sb an unfriendly look ◊ {ethnology} the Bai national minority ◊ Bai (surname) ◊ say, state, explain ◊ {theatre} spoken parts (in a Chinese opera, etc.) ◊ {linguistics} (of Chinese text) written wrong or mispronounced ◊ dialect ◊ spoken (language), vernacular ◊ colloquial (vs literary)

百 bǎi ◊ hundred, 100; hundredfold ◊ numerous, all kinds of, all sorts of ◊ Bai (surname)

帮助 bāngzhù ◊ help, assist ◊ help, assistance

报纸 bàozhǐ ◊ newspaper ◊ newsprint

比 bǐ ◊ compare ◊ than ◊ to (in a score, e.g., sān bǐ èr 三比二 "3 to 2") ◊ emulate, compete, match ◊ gesture, gesticulate ◊ ratio, proportion ◊ draw an analogy (with), liken (to), compare ◊ copy, model after ◊ {regional} aim at, direct towards ◊ {classical} close to, next to ◊ {classical} cling to, collude with ◊ {classical} recently

别 bié ◊ other, another, different ◊ depart, leave, separate ◊ {regional} change, turn around ◊ distinguish, differentiate ◊ distinction, difference ◊ category, type ◊ stick into, obstruct (sb/sth) ◊ trip (sb), cause to stumble ◊ block (another bike or other vehicle with one's own) ◊ (contraction of the prohibitive bùyào 不要) "don't...!" ◊ Bie (surname)

宾馆 bīnguǎn ◊ hotel, guesthouse

C

长 cháng ◊ long; length ◊ (one's) strong point(s), forte ◊ be good at sth, be strong in sth ◊ surplus, spare, extra (in this meaning, formerly pronounced zhàng)

唱歌 chànggē ◊ sing, sing a song

出 chū ◊ go out, exit, come out, come from ◊ give out, issue, offer ◊ occur, happen, arise, emerge, show, appear ◊ produce, turn out, yield ◊ publish ◊ vent (like one's anger) ◊ expend, pay (out), spend ◊ {measure word} (used for theatrical or acrobatic performances, plays, readings, etc.) ◊ {regional} (suffix indicating direction of movement) ◊ (as verb ending) out

穿 chuān ◊ penetrate, pierce (through) ◊ pass through, go through, cross ◊ wear, put on (clothing), have... on, be dressed in ◊ to thread, string (like pearls, beads, etc.) ◊ {grammar} (verbal complement used after certain action verbs to indicate that the action was thorough and complete [e.g., kànchuān 看穿 "see through"])

次 cì ◊ order, sequence, position (in a sequence),... times ◊ arrangement ◊ the following, second, next ◊ sub- (as in cìdàlù 次大陸/次大陆 "subcontinent") ◊ second-rate, inferior, shoddy, substandard, of low(er) quality ◊ {written} stopover, lay-over ◊ among, between, in the middle of ◊ {measure word}... time(s) (following a numeral, used for number of occurrences/times/occasions) ◊ Ci (surname) ◊ {chem} hypo-

从 cóng ◊ from ◊ through, since, by ◊ ever (before negation, e.g., cóng méiyǒu 從沒有/从没有) ◊ always (usually followed by 不, 沒/没, 未 etc. to mean "never") ◊ follow, accompany ◊ comply, conform, follow, obey ◊ act in a certain way (e.g., cóngkuān 從寬/从宽 "treat with leniency") ◊ attendant, footman, follower ◊ secondary ◊ cousin (relationship based on having the same paternal ancestor) ◊ Cong (surname)

错 cuò ◊ wrong, mistaken, erroneous ◊ mistake, error, fault ◊ interlocking, inlaid, intricate ◊ stagger, alternate (like office hours, shifts) ◊ (preceded by a negation like bù 不) bad (bùcuò 不錯/不错 means "not bad", or "very good") ◊ {regional} except, with the exception of, but for... ◊ {written} inlay (with gold, silver, etc.) ◊ {tool} a grindstone for polishing jade ◊ polish jade

D

打 dǎ ◊ strike, hit, beat ◊ break, smash, wreck ◊ batter, attack, fight ◊ come into contact with, deal with (as in dǎ jiāodao 打交道 "have dealings with") ◊ build, construct ◊ forge (like a knife) ◊ pack (like luggage) ◊ apply (like paint) ◊ make (like a phone call) ◊ remove (as in the medical term dǎchóng 打蟲/打虫 "deworm") ◊ knit, weave ◊ take/board (a train, plane) ◊ take/get/hire (a taxi) ◊ ladle, fetch (like porridge, water) ◊ hunt/catch (as in dǎyú 打魚/打鱼 "catch fish") ◊ shoot (with a fire-arm) ◊ collect, gather (like firewood) ◊ draft (a document, estimate, etc.) ◊ do (like odd jobs) ◊ label as, charge with ◊ fight (a war, battle) ◊ play (a game, sport) ◊ buy ◊ be about, concern ◊ {colloquial} (used like cóng 從/从) from; (used like cóng 從/从... qǐ 起) beginning at...

篮球 lánqiú ◊ basketball (the game or the ball itself)

大家 dàjiā ◊ everybody, everyone, all of us/you (often used in reference to the members of an audience, etc.) ◊ (after the pronouns nǐmen 你們/你们, wǒmen 我們/我们, zánmen 咱們/咱们, or tāmen 他們/他们:) all of (you/us/them) ◊ master, authority, expert ◊ a powerful family

到 dào ◊ (from...) to, up until, up to...; as of ◊ arrive, reach ◊ (preceding a location) (go) to, leave for ◊ successfully..., succeed in...(verbal suffix indicating success of the verb's action, as in kàndào 看到 "get to see, notice") ◊ thorough, thoughtful, considerate ◊ Dao (surname)

得 de ◊ {grammar} (as structural particle between verb/adjective and a following complement) able to...; to the degree of...(used after certain verbs to indicate ability, possibility, or achievement to a certain degree, e.g., wǒ kàn de hěn qīngchu 我看得很清楚 "I could see it clearly")

等 děng ◊ wait (for), await ◊ until, by the time when..., by the time that... ◊ {measure word} (used for grade, rank, class, degree) ◊ a (certain) kind, type, sort ◊ equal (to), similar ◊ {grammar} (plural suffix) ◊ and so on/forth/etc. ◊ {grammar} (used to indicate the end of an enumeration of items in a series)

弟弟 dìdi ◊ younger brother

第一 dì-yī ◊ first ◊ primary, most important

懂 dǒng ◊ know, understand (like a language, what has been said, etc.) ◊ comprehend

对 duì ◊ toward, to, facing, regarding ◊ be directed at, confront, treat, cope with ◊ opposite ◊ couple, pair (usually a man and a woman) ◊ {measure word}... pair(s) of... (used for things that come in pairs, like shoes, or for abstract dualities, as in yī duì máodùn 一對矛盾/一对矛盾 "a contradiction") ◊ agree, fit ◊ compare, identify, check ◊ set, adjust, synchronize (like clocks) ◊ pair up, fit together, coordinate ◊ correct, right ◊ adulterate, mix with, add, dilute (like wine with water) ◊ split in half (like profit) ◊ {literature, poetry} couplet

F

房间 fángjiān ◊ room (of a house, etc.)
非常 fēicháng ◊ extraordinary, unusual ◊ very, extremely
服务员 fúwùyuán ◊ attendant, service person

G

高 gāo ◊ high, tall (in contrast to dī 低 "low"); height ◊ (of quality, etc.) above average, top, superior, advanced ◊ of high(er) rank/degree/level ◊ (of sound) (too) loud/sharp/high ◊ {honorific} your, his/her, their (opinion, etc.) ◊ old, aged ◊ expensive, dear ◊ {colloquial, new usage} tipsy/drunk, "high" (on alcohol or drugs) (a literal translation of English "high") ◊ {chem} (of a chemical compound) "high-oxygen"; containing one more oxygen atom (as in gāoměngsuānjiǎ 高錳酸鉀/高锰酸钾 "potassium permanganate") ◊ {math, geometry} the altitude (like of a triangle) ◊ Gao (surname)
告诉 gàosu ◊ tell, inform
哥哥 gēge ◊ elder brother
给 gěi ◊ give, hand (to), present, grant ◊ (after a verb indicating transfer) to, toward; for, for the benefit of ◊ let, allow (also used as an emphatic particle, mainly in passive-voice sentences)
公共汽车 gōnggòngqìchē ◊ bus
公司 gōngsī ◊ company, corporation, firm
贵 guì ◊ expensive, costly, high-priced ◊ valuable, precious ◊ noble, of high status, of high rank, honorable ◊ {formal, honorific} your (surname, company etc.) ◊ (short for Guìzhōu 贵州/贵州) Guizhou Province ◊ Gui (surname)
过 guò ◊ go past, pass (by), go through, cross ◊ exceed, go beyond ◊ mistake ◊ blame or criticize sb for a mistake ◊ transfer (like money), adopt (like a child) ◊ read, go over, recall, call to mind ◊ {written} visit, stop by ◊ {regional} pass away, die ◊ {grammar} outperform, or fail (following dé 得 or bù 不 after a verb) ◊ {chem} per-, super- ◊ {regional} be contagious, infect ◊ Guo (surname)

H

还 hái ◊ still, yet ◊ still more, even more ◊ also, as well, too, in addition, furthermore ◊ (when preceding an adjective indicating acceptable quality) passably, fairly, rather... ◊ (in rhetorical questions) even..., if... ◊ in spite of (sth unexpected, a difficulty, etc.) ◊ (to express emphasis) really, very ◊ (as a particle indicating grudging acceptance or unexpectedness) well then...

孩子 háizi ◊ child ◊ children

好吃 hǎochī ◊ delicious, tasty ("good to eat")

黑 hēi ◊ (of colour) black, dark ◊ secret (often illicit), shady, unlawful, clandestine ◊ evil, wicked, sinister, vicious ◊ unethical, reactionary, counter-revolutionary ◊ {colloquial} do sth unethical or unlawful ◊ (short for Hēilóngjiāng 黑龍江/黑龙江) Heilongjiang Province ◊ Hei (surname)

红 hóng ◊ red (colour) ◊ {informal} be popular, be "hot", be in great demand ◊ red cloth (hung to symbolize festive occasions, success, happiness, good luck, etc.) ◊ {figurative} (politically) "red" (i.e. Communist, socialist-minded, revolutionary) ◊ {economics} dividend, bonus ◊ (symbol of success) ◊ Hong (surname)

火车站 huǒchēzhàn ◊ train station

J

机场 jīchǎng ◊ airport

鸡蛋 jīdàn ◊ (hen's) egg

件 jiàn ◊ {measure word}... piece(s) of..., item (used for clothing items, pieces of luggage, implements, utensils, matters, law cases, incidents, etc.) ◊ letter, document, piece of correspondence ◊ case (of bundled goods, such as soft drinks) ◊ {pottery/porcelain manufacturing} (standard measure for clay, used for measuring the size of vases)

教室 jiàoshì ◊ classroom

姐姐 jiějie ◊ elder sister ◊ elder sister (form of address for a female relative of the same generation, but older than oneself)

介绍 jièshào ◊ introduce, present; introduction ◊ recommend, suggest ◊ introduce, give an account of, brief (sb about sth); introduction, briefing

进 jìn ◊ advance, move forward/ahead (opposite of tuì 退) ◊ enter, come/go in ◊ take in, bring in, receive ◊ recruit, admit ◊ submit, present ◊ eat, drink, take ◊ (as verb ending) into, in ◊ {measure word} (of an old-style residential compound with an inner courtyard or multiple linked courtyards) a courtyard and its associated rooms ◊ {sports} goal (in soccer) ◊ {Chinese chess} advance (a number of points)

近 jìn ◊ near (in time or space, in contrast to yuǎn 遠/远 "far, distant") ◊ close, intimate ◊ simple, easy to understand ◊ nearly, approximately

就 jiù ◊ then, in that case ◊ on the subject of, with regard to, concerning, regarding, in connection with, as far as (sth is concerned) ◊ approach, move towards ◊ take up, enter upon, start doing (sth) ◊ comply with, yield to ◊ avail oneself of (sth at hand) ◊ at once, right away, in a moment ◊ (adverb indicating that a preceding number/quantity/time is relatively small/few/early) as early as, as long ago as, as soon as, as much/many as ◊ exactly, precisely ◊ only, merely, just, nothing (or no one) else than ◊ even if ◊ accomplish (sometimes used as a verbal resultative ending)

觉得juéde ◊ feel (like tired) ◊ think, believe

K

咖啡kāfēi ◊ coffee

开始kāishǐ ◊ begin, start ◊ set about, set out on ◊ beginning, initial phase

考试kǎoshì ◊ exam ◊ test ◊ take an exam or test

可能kěnéng ◊ possible, probable, likely ◊ may, maybe, probably ◊ possibly ◊ probability, possibility, likelihood

可以kěyǐ ◊ may, can ◊ passable, not bad, pretty good ◊ be worth (doing)

课 kè ◊ lesson, class ◊ {measure word} (for a lesson, unit of a textbook, etc.) ◊ administrative unit in certain organizations ◊ taxes ◊ levy, collect (taxes)

快 kuài ◊ fast ◊ hurry up ◊ soon, shortly ◊ keen, sharp (-witted, etc.) ◊ content, happy ◊ Kuai (surname)

快乐kuàilè ◊ happy, joyful, cheerful, delightful

L

累 lèi ◊ tired, exhausted, fatigued, weary ◊ fatigue, weariness, strain ◊ work hard, toil

离 lí ◊ distance (between, from) ◊ (following distance measure)... distant (from) ◊ leave, go away ◊ lacking, without ◊ Li (one of the Eight Trigrams in the Yìjīng 易經/易经 "Book of Changes") ◊ cut, sever ◊ meet with, encounter ◊ set out, display ◊ experience ◊ bright ◊ {musical instrument} li (large qín 琴 [guitar/zither]) ◊ Li (surname)

两 liǎng ◊ two, both (sides, parties, etc.) ◊ liang (Chinese ounce, equal to 50 grams) ◊ tael (unit of silver) ◊ liang (unit of 25 soldiers)

零 líng ◊ zero, 0, nought, nil ◊ fragments, remnants ◊ fragmentary, fractional ◊ odd (number, amount, etc.) ◊ (on a thermometer) zero (degrees) ◊ (of leaves, etc.) wither and fall ◊ light rain ◊ Ling (surname)

路 lù ◊ road, path, way; means, approach ◊ line, train (like of reasoning, thought) ◊ route, line ◊ Lu (administrative region during the Song, Jin and Yuan Dynasties) ◊ Lu (surname)

旅游 lǚyóu ◊ tourism ◊ traveling as a tourist ◊ travel, trip

M

卖 mài ◊ sell (opposite of mǎi 買/买 "buy, purchase"); sell out, betray ◊ outgoing, not holding back ◊ show off ◊ {measure word} (used for an order in a restaurant)

慢 màn ◊ slow (in contrast to kuài 快 "fast") ◊ postpone, defer ◊ haughty, arrogant, rude ◊ smear, daub ◊ {archaic} Man (name of a melody during the Tang and Song dynasties)

忙 máng ◊ (be) busy ◊ hurriedly, hurry to, hasten to ◊ Mang (surname)

每 měi ◊ each, every ◊ every time, whenever ◊ Mei (surname)

妹妹 mèimei ◊ younger sister ◊ younger female cousin ◊ female relative of the same generation and clan but younger than oneself

门 mén ◊ door, entrance, gate ◊ switch, valve ◊ hole/opening in human body ◊ family ◊ school (of thought), (religious) sect ◊ a teacher's or master's entrance hall ◊ means, method, key ◊ category ◊ {biology} phylum (of animals or plants) ◊ -gate (used by the media to create new words referring to a scandal, after the pattern of Shuǐmén [Shìjiàn] 水門 [事件]/水门 [事件] "Watergate") ◊ {measure word}... course(s) of..., ... subject(s) of..., ... skill(s) of... (used for school courses, skills, branches or subjects of knowledge, etc.) ◊ {measure word} (used for cannons) ◊ {measure word} (used for relatives, marriages, families related by marriage, etc.) ◊ Men (surname)

面条 miàntiáo ◊ noodles

N

男 nán ◊ man; male ◊ son ◊ baron (title in European nobility) ◊ baron (the fifth of the five ranks of nobility in feudal China of the past) ◊ Nan (surname)

您 nín ◊ you (polite form) (can be plural in certain contexts, as in 您二位 nín èr wèi "the two of you")

牛奶 niúnǎi ◊ (cow's) milk

女 nǚ ◊ woman, female ◊ girl, daughter ◊ {Chinese astronomy} Nü (Nǚ Xiù 女宿 "Nü constellation", one of the Èrshíbā Xiù 二十八宿 "28 Lunar Mansions of the Chinese zodiac")

P

旁边 pángbiān ◊ side; on the side

跑步 pǎobù ◊ run ◊ jog ◊ jogging

便宜 piányi ◊ cheap, inexpensive ◊ benefit, advantage (mostly unexpected, uncalled for, or undeserved) ◊ let (sb) get off easy (like without punishment), let (sb) get away with sth too easily ◊ let (sb) make off with (an undeserved benefit)

票 piào ◊ ticket ◊ ballot, vote ◊ bank note, (dollar, etc.) bill ◊ hostage held for ransom

Q

妻子 qīzi ◇ wife
起床 qǐchuáng ◇ get up, rise (in the morning), get out of bed
千 qiān ◇ thousand, 1,000 ◇ thousands, great many ◇ kilo- ◇ Qian (surname)
铅笔 qiānbǐ ◇ pencil
晴 qíng ◇ (of weather) clear, fine
去年 qùnián ◇ last year

R

让 ràng ◇ let, allow ◇ have or make (sb do sth), cause ◇ yield, give in, give up ◇ yield for, give (the right of) way to (e.g., another vehicle, pedestrians) ◇ let sb else have sth ◇ {sound transcription} Jean (French given name)
日 rì ◇ sun ◇ day, daytime ◇ daily, on a daily basis, every day ◇ the days, time ◇ (short for Rìběn 日本) Japan; Japanese

S

上班 shàngbān ◇ go to work ◇ start work, go on duty
身体 shēntǐ ◇ the body ◇ one's health
生病 shēngbìng ◇ be taken ill, fall ill
生日 shēngrì ◇ birthday ◇ date of birth
时间 shíjiān ◇ time
事情 shìqing ◇ matter, affair, thing, event
手表 shǒubiǎo ◇ wristwatch, watch
手机 shǒujī ◇ mobile phone, cellular phone, cell phone
说话 shuōhuà ◇ speak, talk, chat ◇ gossip ◇ blame, reproach ◇ before you can say, in no time ◇ words ◇ shuohua (storytelling during the Sòng 宋 Dynasty)
送 sòng ◇ give as a present ◇ send, deliver ◇ accompany (like a guest to the door)
虽然 suīrán ◇ although, though ◇ although it is so
但是 dànshì ◇ but, still, yet

T

它 tā ◇ it (third person singular, neuter) ◇ other, another
踢 tī ◇ kick (like playing soccer) ◇ alarmed, frightened
足球 zúqiú ◇ football, soccer (the game or the ball itself)
题 tí ◇ forehead ◇ topic, subject ◇ title, heading ◇ write, inscribe
跳舞 tiàowǔ ◇ dance

W

外 wài ◊ outside, foreign ◊ except for, other than (often preceded by a phrase with chú 除……) ◊ unofficial (like history)

完 wán ◊ finish (the action of the preceding verb) ◊ Wan (surname)

玩 wán ◊ play ◊ play with ◊ have fun, relax, enjoy oneself ◊ gaming

晚上 wǎnshang ◊ in the evening, at night ◊ evening, night

往 wǎng ◊ go, go to ◊ towards, in the direction of ◊ past, former, previous, earlier

为什么 wèishénme ◊ why

问 wèn ◊ ask, inquire ◊ send one's regards, inquire after (sb's health etc.) ◊ Wen (surname)

问题 wèntí ◊ question, problem, issue ◊ crux, key, heart ◊ mishap, trouble, accident

X

西瓜 xīguā ◊ watermelon, Citrullus lanatus (the plant or its fruit) ‖ (Beijing colloquial pronunciation: xīgua)

希望 xīwàng ◊ hope (to/that), wish (to/that), desire to, want to ◊ a wish, hope, expectation, possibility, promise (of)

洗 xǐ ◊ wash, bathe, rinse, clean ◊ {religion} baptize ◊ remedy, redress, (set) right ◊ eliminate, get rid of, clear away ◊ kill and loot, sack (like a city) ◊ {photography} develop (a film) ◊ erase, delete ◊ shuffle (like deck of cards) ◊ small container for washing writing brushes

小时 xiǎoshí ◊ hour

笑 xiào ◊ smile, laugh ◊ ridicule, deride

新 xīn ◊ new ◊ modern, contemporary ◊ recently married ◊ newly, recently, lately ◊ Xin (surname)

姓 xìng ◊ surname, family or clan name ◊ the populace ◊ officials (in general)

休息 xiūxi ◊ rest, take a rest/break ◊ relax ◊ go to bed, retire ◊ a rest/break

雪 xuě ◊ snow ◊ colour or luster of snow ◊ wipe away (shame, etc.), avenge ◊ Xue (surname)

Y

颜色 yánsè ◊ colour ◊ facial expression

眼睛 yǎnjing ◊ eye

羊肉 yángròu ◊ mutton

药 yào ◊ medicine, drugs, pharmaceuticals ◊ various chemicals (like gunpowder, solder, etc.) ◊ cure with drugs ◊ poison, kill (like rats, insects) ◊ {bot} Chinese herbaceous peony, Paeonia lactiflora ◊ Yao (surname)

要 yào ◊ want, need, desire ◊ demand, ask for, request ◊ must ◊ will, be going to ◊ need to, should ◊ it is necessary that..., one must... ◊ if ◊ if one hopes to..., in order to... ◊ (used in comparisons, for example 要比... yào bǐ or 比...要... bǐ...yào...), expresses a judgment/evaluation or highlights the difference ◊ important ◊ suppose that..., if, in case ◊ (yào..., yào...) either..., or.... ◊ Yāo (surname)

也 yě ◊ also, too, as well ◊ (followed by a negative) (not) even ◊ nevertheless, still

一起 yīqǐ ◊ together ◊ in company, in unison ◊ from the outset ◊ all told, in all ◊ in the same place

一下 yīxià ◊ (used after a verb as its complement, indicates doing sth a short duration, or trying to do sth) ◊ (used after a verb as its complement, indicates a single occurrence of the action of the verb) once, one time ◊ a short while; in a short while; all at once, suddenly ◊ in one fell swoop, at one stroke, in one go

已经 yǐjīng ◊ already

意思 yìsi ◊ meaning, idea, thought ◊ opinion, wish, desire ◊ (a gift, etc. given as) an expression of one's kind feelings, a token (of affection, appreciation, etc.) ◊ suggestion, indication, hint, sign ◊ interest, appeal, fun ◊ do sth as a token

因为 yīnwèi ◊ because, on account of, for ‖ (often pronounced yīnwei)

所以 suǒyǐ ◊ therefore (a conjunction indicating cause-effect relationship) ◊ so ◊ that's why ◊ that's the reason ◊ (same meaning as zhī suǒyǐ 之所以:) the reason that... (often followed by shì yīnwèi 是因為,是因为... "is because...")

阴 yīn ◊ {philosophy, Chinese med} Yin (the female or negative principle in nature, the opposite of yáng 陽/阳) ◊ the moon ◊ the north side of a hill ◊ the south side of a river ◊ {meteorology} overcast, cloudy ◊ shade (of a tree, etc.) ◊ the back side ◊ concave ◊ in intaglio ◊ covert, hidden, secret, inward, underhand ◊ gloomy ◊ sinister, perfidious ◊ of the netherworld, otherworldly ◊ {physics} negative ◊ {physiology} the female genitalia ◊ Yin (surname)

游泳 yóuyǒng ◊ swim

右边 yòubian ◊ right (hand) side

鱼 yú ◊ (a) fish ◊ Yu (surname) ◊ (a propitious symbol as homophone of yú 餘/余 "surplus, abundance")

远 yuǎn ◊ far, distant, remote (in space/time) ◊ (of blood relationship, relatives) distant ◊ (of difference) far, by far ◊ not intimate, distant ◊ Yuan (surname)

运动 yùndòng ◊ sports ◊ physical exercise ◊ motion ◊ movement, campaign, drive ‖ (in the pronunciation "yùndong": campaign, canvass, wangle support)

Z

再 zài ◊ again, once more ◊ further, more ◊ time and again, repeatedly ◊ no matter how... (followed by an adjective or verb, usually with dōu 都 or yě 也 in the following clause)

早上 zǎoshang ◊ in the morning ◊ (early) morning

丈夫 zhàngfu ◊ husband

找 zhǎo ◊ search, seek, look for, try to find ◊ want to see (sb), call on, approach, ask for ◊ give change (money)

着 zhe ◊ {grammar} (verb suffix, comparable to "-ing", indicating that an action is in progress); be -ing (used to indicate a state that is presently in existence and ongoing [e.g., mén kāizhe 門開著/门开着 "the door is open"]) ◊ (used after verbs or adjectives to make them more emphatic in meaning)... indeed ◊ (used as a suffix to form certain prepositions) (like shùnzhe 順著/顺着 "along", cháozhe 朝著/朝着 "facing, towards", etc.)

真 zhēn ◊ real, true, genuine ◊ really, truly ◊ sincere ◊ Zhen (surname)

正在 zhèngzài ◊ (be) in the process of (doing sth), be -ing

知道 zhīdao ◊ know, understand, be aware of, realize; know of; learn (of), find out

准备 zhǔnbèi ◊ prepare, make ready ◊ plan, intend

走 zǒu ◊ walk, travel on foot ◊ run ◊ move, shift ◊ leave, depart ◊ (verb ending) ...away ◊ run away, flee, escape ◊ leak (out) ◊ lose the original shape, flavour, etc. ◊ through, from

最 zuì ◊ (the) most..., -est (prefix for the superlative, e.g., zuìdà 最大 "biggest")

左边 zuǒbian ◊ the left side

汉语水平考试

语法点

Grammar Points

HSK Grammar Language Points

HSK Level 2

The presentation of grammar points for HSK Level 2 is based upon the curricular outline in:

HSK 考试大纲, HSK Level 2, pp. 12-14. Published by the Confucius Institute Headquarters (Hanban). People's Education Press, Peking 2015.
ISBN: 978-7-107-30419-4

There are 12 Language Grammar Point topics with eventual sub-divisions, all of which are listed on the following page.

Overview

Words and Phrases

1. Verbs
1.1 离
1.2 会
1.3 可以
1.4 要
1.5 看看
1.6 看一看
1.7 运动运动
1.8 Verbal complement of result used as an attribute

2. Pronouns: 为什么？

3. Adjectives
3.1 多
3.2 红红

4. Measure Words
4.1 多 following a noun phrase numeral + measure word
4.2 次
4.3 件件
4.4 一下

5. Adverbs
5.1 都
5.2 Use of 还
5.3 就
5.4 也
5.5 已经
5.6 有一点儿
5.7 再
5.8 真
5.9 最

6. Prepositions
6.1 从
6.2 对
6.3 往

7. Particles

7.1 吧
7.2 的 phrase
7.3 得
7.4 过
7.5 了 at the end of a sentence
7.6 着

Sentences

8. Special Sentence Patterns
8.1 是。。。的
8.2 让
8.3 Sentences of Comparison with 比

9. Types of Sentences
9.1 Ques*tion Sentences with Yes/No Answer* 26
9.2 "Alternative" Question Sentence
9.3 Exclamation Sentence with 真
9.4 Using 别 and 不要。。。了

Complements

10. Complements
10.1 Complement of Result
10.2 Complement of Potentiality
10.3 Complement of Degree
10.4 Complement of Quantity
10.5 Complement of Direction: Simple Complements of Direction

Complex Sentence Structures

11. Complex Sentences
11.1 虽然。。。，但是。。
11.2 因为。。。，所以。。

Fixed Structures

12. Fixed Structures
12.1 要/快/快要/就要。。。了
12.2 在/正在/正。。。呢

Suggestions For Further Reading

Words and Phrases

1. Verbs

1.1 离
In the sample sentence below, 离 functions similar to a preposition of location before a place noun with a predicate complex following the prepositional phrase:

他的家离学校很远。
离 is placed before 学校 as a place of destination while 他的家 is the place of departuire. In this case, 离 may be simply translated with *to*:

From his home to his school (it) is very/quite far.

Chinese grammar treats 离 as a verb with several shades of meaning. In the sample sentence above, it actually behaves like a preposition in a prepositional phrase placed before the predicate complex 很远.

> **General observations on the use of 很 before a predicative adjective like 远:**
> 远 belongs to the semantic category of relative adjectives. Relative adjectives can have comparisons like *He is taller than me* or *He is the tallest of us all*. Other examples of relative adjectives in English and Chinese are good, bad, great, big, small, far, etc. There are also absolute adjectives like red or other colour adjectives that cannot be compared in the same way like relative adjectives. In Chinese grammar, relative adjectives must always be preceded by 很; if not, it would give them a sense of comparison like *taller*, etc. 很 is not placed before adjectives with an absolute sense of meaning.

1.2 会
会 is a modal verb often placed before another main verb in a sentence to express either the ability of a skill acquired or possibility in addition to other shades of meaning. In the sample sentence below

今天可能会下雨。

the context clearly suggests that it expresses possibility and a future state.

1.3 可以
This is another modal verb commonly translated into English as "can", "may" (the latter in the sense of permission). In the sample sentences below:

(1) 你在写什么？我可以看看吗？
(2) 我觉得住在这儿很好，离学校很近，我可以每天走着去上学。

可以 in (1) indicates the sense of permission, 可以 in (2) indicates "being able to do something" because of favourable circumstances.

1.4 要

要 is a modal verb indicating different senses of modality such as "want" or "should".

(1) 每天早上她都要慢跑一个小时。
(2) 他生病了，要多喝水，多休息。

In the two sample sentences above, 要 in (1) indicates desire while 要 in (2) may be translated as "should" or "must".

1.5 看看

Doubled monosyllabic verbs can express an intensive act of short duration. This is also suggested by the context of the sample sentence below:

这本书不错，你可以看看。

1.6 看一看

Some doubled verbs like 看看 in 1.5 may also have 一 inserted between them.
In the sample sentence below:

这本书不错，你可以读一读。

读一读 expresses a similar notion of intensive but brief action like 看看 in 1.5 above.

1.7 运动运动

运动 is a verb consisting of more than one syllable. In such a case, in the case of reduplication, its parts appear reduplicated according to the pattern ABAB as the sample sentence below suggests:

外面天气很好，我们出去运动运动？

1.8 Verbal complement of result used as an attribute

This entails a somewhat more complex structure as indicated in the sentence sample below:

我丈夫<u>新買</u>的紅茶，你來一杯？

Here, 新買 is in attributive relationship to 紅茶 indicated by 的 before 紅茶 as a head noun. 買 functions here as a verbal complement of result (remember that in Chinese grammar, adjectives are considered verb-like elements).

2. Pronouns: 为什么？

为什么 asks for a reason of doing something and is commonly translated with "why" in English. Note that 为什么 literally translates as "for what (reason)?". This is also suggested by context of the sample sentence below:

3. Adjectives

3.1 多

多 is an adjective and is listed in the 《新华字典》 with the following shades of meaning:

1. many, much (adjective),
2. to what an extent (adverb, used in exclamations).

Here is a small activity assignment:

> Determine the grammatical role of 多 according to sentence context in the sample sentence below:
>
> 多穿件衣服。
>
> Is it (1) or (2)?

3.2 红红

红红 is an instance of adjectives that can be reduplicated like verbs in Chinese. From sentence context in the sample sentence below, you may well conclude that there is an apple that looks really tasty to eat:

这个苹果红红的，真好吃。

4. Measure Words

General Observations: You will certainly be aware that measure words such as 个 or 本 are required to be put before nouns in when a demonstrative pronoun or a numeral precedes the head noun. Measure words then as a rule are put between demonstrative pronoun/numeral and the head word modified in a phrase. Certain nouns require certain measure words in Chinese, for example: 本 is a measure word for words like 书 while a noun like 人 would require 个 as a measure word to be inserted.

4.1 多 following a noun phrase with a measure word
In the sample sentence below:

这个电影很长，有两个多小时。

多 here indicates that the film was over two hours of duration and hence must be translated as "over…" or "more than…" 多 in such a case always follows directly the measure word but precedes the head noun.

4.2 次
There are also measure words for verbs or verbal phrases indicating, for example, frequency of action. 次 preceded by a numeral is equivalent to "times" in English as the context of the sample sentence below suggests:

医生说，这个药每天吃三次。

4.3 件件
件件 is an instance of measure words reduplicated indicating a sense of meaning like "every" or "all". This would also apply to the context suggested by the sample sentence below:

这个商店的衣服件件很漂亮。

4.4 一下
一下 is another instance of a verbal measure word, and from the context of the sample sentence below it is suggested that its meaning is something like "just" or "for a moment":

你读一下这几个汉字。

5. Adverbs

5.1 都
都 is an adverb; in combination with nouns it is often translated as "all" in English. Note that word classes differ in both English and Chinese: in English, "all" is a quantifier preceding a noun directly; in Chinese, 都 always precedes a verbal element while it can never precede a noun.

For 都, the following shades of meaning are listed in Chinese dictionaries:

1. completely
2. *(used for emphasis)* even, already

Which function does 都 have in the sample sentence below - (1) or (2)?

都这么晚了，你可能不会打电话了。

5.2 Use of 还
First, consider the sample sentences below:

A. 已经晚上10点了，你还在教室里学习。
B. 他昨天来过，明天还来。
C. 我们玩儿得很高兴，还学会了一些汉语。

Here is a list of possible English translational equivalents for 还:

1. still, yet
2. also, too
3. passable, fairly

Study Activity:
Which of these possible English meaning definitions can be assigned to sample sentences A - C according to their respective sentence contexts?

5.3 就
就 is an adverb that sometimes can be translated as "then" in English; it depends all on the actual sentence context.

Consider the following sentence samples below:

(A) 从这儿去火车公共汽车20分钟就到了。
(B) 报纸就电视旁边。

The 《新华字典》 lists the following meaning shades for 就:

1. come near, move towards
2. engage in, enter upon
3. with 'regard to, taking advantage of
4. be eaten with, go with
5. accomplish, make
6. (adverb) a. expressing an affirmative, emphasize
            b. in that case
            c. at once, right away
            d. merely
7. (conjunction) even if

> For the use of 就, also compare 《外国人实用汉语语法》, pp. 111- 116.

For the two sample sentences above, which of the English meaning definitions apply according to sentence context?

5.4 也
也 means "also", "too" as the following sentences suggest:

A：我喜欢这件黑色的。
B: 我也喜欢， 但是它不便宜。

5.5 已经
已经 means "already" as suggested by the context of the sample sentence below:
现在已经12点了。

5.6 有一点儿
有一点儿 means "a bit/ a little" as suggested by the context of the sample sentence below:

我这两天有一点儿忙。

5.7 再
再 means "again" as suggested by the context of the sentence samples below:

这个手机能再便宜一些吗？
服务员， 我们想再要一个菜。

5.8 真
真 means "truly/really", see the sentence sample below:

你今天买的东西真不少。

5.9 最
最 means "most as suggested by the context of the sample sentence below:

服务员， 你们这儿什么菜最好吃？

6. Prepositions

6.1 从

从 means "from". Compare its use in the sample sentences below:

我从11岁开始踢足球，已经踢了10年了。
从学校到机场，坐出租车要一个小时。

6.2 对

对 means "for" in contexts such as those in the sample sentence below:

医生说，多吃苹果对身体好。

6.3 往

往 means "in the direction of/towards" as a preposition; as an adverb 往往, it may mean also "often". Which shade of meaning does apply to 往 in the sample sentence below?

我正往学校呢，你们等我几分钟。

7. Particles

7.1 吧
吧 as a sentence-final particle and indicates request, command, consultation or proposal. Which of these modal senses expressed by 吧 do apply according to context in the sentence samples below? For further details, cf. 《外国人实用汉语语法》, pp. 142.

I. 这件衣服真漂亮，很贵吧？
II. 生病了，就别去学校了，在家休息吧。
III. A: 我可以明天去吗？
　　B: 好吧。

7.2 的 phrase
The 的 phrase in the sample below functions as a substantivised adjectival phrase:

我想买手机，你看这个红的怎么样？

7.3 得
得 after a verb indicates degree or extent of an action. There are other uses as well that do not apply regarding the context of the sample sentence below:

这本书写得真有意思。

How can you translate this sentence into English then?

7.4 过
过 indicates aspect of something already experienced as the context of the sample sentence below suggests:

我看过那个电影，还不错。

Try a translation of this sample sentence yourself.

7.5 了 at the end of a sentence
了 at the end of a sentence indicates a change of state. Try to translate the sample sentence below accordingly to this sentence context:

我生病了。

7.6 着
着 after a verb indicates duration or continuation of an ongoing action. For the use of 着, cf. the contexts of the sample sentences below:

有什么事吗？我真忙着呢。
爸爸每天走着去公司。

Sentences

8. Special Sentence Patterns

8.1 是。。。的
We have briefly dealt with the emphatic frame structure 是。。。的 in the Grammar Guide Notes for HSK Level 1. Here is another instance of using it. Here, it is an entire sentence that is "embedded":

是<u>张惶先生帮助我</u>的。

8.2 让
让 here is a verb used in a causative sense (causing someone to do something somewhere) in form of a pivotal sentence structure:

公司<u>让他去中国工作</u>。

8.3 Sentences of Comparison with 比
a) A + 比 + B + Adjective/ A 比 B +形容词
今年比去年冷。

b) A + 比 + B + other elements /A比B+形容词+其他
他比我大三岁。

c) A + 比 + B + Adjective + 多了 / A比B+形容词+多了
那儿非常冷，比北京冷多了。

9 Types of Sentences

9.1 Question Sentences with Yes/No Answer / 是非问句
对不起，在等我们10分钟，<u>好吗</u>？

9.3 "Alternative" Question Sentence / 正反问句
外面是不是下雨了？

9.3 Exlamation Sentence with 真
你的歌唱得真不错！

9.4 Using 别 and 不要。。。了
Compare the following sentences below:

你别睡了，快起床！
不要说话了， 快睡觉吧。

Both sentence patterns indicate that the speaker shouldn't do a certain thing. Using 别 is more informal while using 不要。。。了 is more usual in formal situations.

Complements

10. Complements

General Observations: Complements of Result and Complements of Degree logically presuppose an action or the development towards a state that is completed. It is because only after an action is complete or a level of a (new) state has been reached, you cannot assess the result or a degree of action or state.

Complement of result
10.1 Verb + 对/错/到/懂/开/完 / 动词+对/错/到/懂/开/完
这个字你写错了。
我找到我的手表了。
你送我的那本书我已经读完了。

10.2 Complement of Potentiality: Verb + +得/不+见/完/下 / 动词+得/不+见/完/下
字太小了，我看不见。
这么多菜，我们吃得完吗？

10.3 Complement of Degree: Verb + 得+不错/很好 / 动词+得+不错/很好
她非常喜欢唱歌，唱得很好。

General Observation: The verb combined with a complement of degree must be monosyllabic; if it has an object it must be repeated after the complement.

10.4 Complement of Quantity
a) Verb + Complement of Time / 动词+时量补语

这本书他看了<u>三天</u>。

b) Verb + complement of quantity / 动词+动量补语
这个电影我看过<u>三次</u>。

10.5 Complement of Direction: Simple Complement of Direction

General Observation: Certain verbs may have 来 or 去 attached to them as complements with 来 indicating an action in the direction towards where the speaker is and 去 indicating an action in a direction moving away from the speaker's position. In the sample sentence below, 来 is used to indicate that a telephone call was made to the speaker.

是谁打<u>来</u>的电话？

Complex Sentence Structures

General Observations: Complex sentences consist of several combines sentences brought together in a single sentence complex. The immediate constituent parts of a single complex sentence are called "clauses" in English grammar.

Basically, there are two kinds of complex sentences:

● *Coordinate complex sentences.* Their clauses are all independent (simple) sentences that are structurally and semantically well-formed and make sense when being used alone (independently). In Chinese syntax, a special case of coordinate complex sentences are those used with so-called correlatives.

● *Subordinate complex sentences.* They also consist of clauses, but at least one of them cannot be used as an independent sentence and would not make sense when being used alone as for example in *I know that you are a person of integrity*. The underlined clause is subordinate to *I know* and cannot be used by itself.

For more information on the grammar of complex sentences in Chinese, you should consult the following pages in 《外国人实用汉语语法》 for further reading:

- on complex coordinate sentences: pp. 588 - 595.
- on complex coordinate sentences and correlatives: pp. 5156 - 608.
- on subordinate complex sentences: pp. 608 - 645.

11. Complex Sentences

11.1 虽然。。。。,但是。。。
The sample sentence below is a coordinate complex sentence expressing the idea that despite A is in the condition (or state) of X, A nevertheless is also in a state of Y.
A rough English translation of such a complex coordinate sentence may then follow accordingly the following pattern: "Although A is in the state of X, it is nevertheless also in the state of Y" or "A is in the state of Y, it is yet in the state of Y".

Study the context of the sample sentence below:

虽然那块手表很漂亮, 但是太贵了。

11.2   因为。。。,所以。。
In this sort of complex coordinate sentence, there is a condition A expressed in the first clause that will bear an impact on the result B expressed in the second clause.

Study the context of the sample sentence below:

因为天气很冷,所以她没去游泳。

Fixed Structures
固定格式

Fixed Structures such as the ones listed below are standing expression formula often used in colloquial or written language of Chinese or both to express a certain idea. They are difficult to include in a canon of grammar points to be treated otherwise; therefore, they are listed here a separate grammar points.

12. Fixed Structures

12.1 要/快/快要/就要。。。了

This type of fixed structure suggests a sense of immediate future or that something will happen very soon.

Study the context of the sample sentences below and then try to translate them into idiomatic English:

已经10点45了，我要会家了。
船还有十分钟就要开了，你朋友怎么还没到？

12.2 在/正在/正。。。呢

This type of fixed structure suggests a sense of an action still in progress or an ongoing process.

Study the context of the sample sentence below and then try to translate it into idiomatic English:

他还没睡觉，正在床上看电视呢。

Suggestions For Further Reading

外国人实用汉语语法 (A Practical Chinese Grammar for Foreigners), Beijing Language and Culture University Press, Beijing 2014 (2008).

汉英双解新华字典 (Xinhua Dictionary with English Translation), Commercial Press, Beijing 2000.

References

A. 孔子学院总部/国家汉办/**Confucius Institute Headquarters (Hanban)**：
《**HSK考试大纲**》/**HSK Test Syllabus:**

HSK 考试大纲 [HSK Test Syllabus], HSK Level 1, pp. 10-11. Published by the Confucius Institute Headquarters (Hanban). People's Education Press, Peking 2015.
ISBN: 978-7-107-30418-7

HSK 考试大纲, HSK Level 2, pp. 12-14. Published by the Confucius Institute Headquarters (Hanban). People's Education Press, Peking 2015.
ISBN: 978-7-107-30419-4

HSK 考试大纲, HSK Level 3, pp. 14-17. Published by the Confucius Institute Headquarters (Hanban). People's Education Press, Peking 2015.
ISBN: 978-7-107-30420-0

HSK 考试大纲, HSK Level 4, pp. 16-19. Published by the Confucius Institute Headquarters (Hanban). People's Education Press, Peking 2015.
ISBN: 978-7-107-30421-7

HSK 考试大纲, HSK Level 5, pp. 16-18. Published by the Confucius Institute Headquarters (Hanban). People's Education Press, Peking 2015.
ISBN: 978-7-107-30422-4

HSK 考试大纲, HSK Level 6, pp. 16-17. Published by the Confucius Institute Headquarters (Hanban). People's Education Press, Peking 2015.
ISBN: 978-7-107-30487-3

B. Complementary Sources Used:

《外国人实用汉语语法》, Beijing Language and Culture University Press, Peking 2014(2008).

《汉语语法百项讲练(初中级)》 [Chinese Grammar-Broken down into 100 items (Basicand Intermediate Level)], Beijing Language and Culture University Press, Peking 2011

《汉英双解新华字典》 [Xinhua Dictionary with English Translation], Commercial-Press, Peking 2000

吕叔湘 (Lü Shuxiang): 《现代汉语八百词》 [The Eighthundred Words of Modern Chi-nese], Commercial Press, Peking 1988

The Dictionary Definitions are taken from different high-quality databases included in the "Professional Chinese-English Dictionary" software, Version 2.0, downloadable from:
http://www.gelber-kaiser.de/ChinDict/Index.html (Freeware).

Prepare Yourself for the Chinese Language Proficiency Exam (HSK)

Volume II:
Intermediate Chinese Language Difficulty Levels HSK Levels 3 and 4

disserta Verlag 2019

Book ISBN 978-3-95935-505-6
eBook ISBN 978-3-95935-506-3

44,90 € (Print)
34,99 € (eBook)

Paperback, 256 pages

Volume III:
Advanced Chinese Language Difficulty Levels HSK Levels 5 and 6

disserta Verlag 2019

Book ISBN 978-3-95935-507-0
eBook ISBN 978-3-95935-508-7

49,90 € (Print)
34,99 € (eBook)

Paperback, 432 pages

www.ingramcontent.com/pod-product-compliance
Lightning Source LLC
Chambersburg PA
CBHW060420300426
44111CB00018B/2916